David –

You are meaning [?] roles in the church [...] especially in your home where the call for spiritual leadership is the greatest. Hopefully this book will help strengthen you in your calling & especially as patriarch of your home. We love you & admire you so very much. We are so thankful Marilyn has you. Thank you for being so kind & good to us.

Lots of love

Mom & Dad
(Ann) (Bob)

Christmas 1990

THE PERFECT LEADER

THE
PERFECT LEADER
*Following Christ's Example
to Leadership Success*

Eric Stephan and
R. Wayne Pace

Deseret Book Company
Salt Lake City, Utah

Library of Congress Cataloging-in-Publication Data

Stephen, Eric G.
  The perfect leader : following Christ's example to
leadership success / by Eric G. Stephan and R. Wayne Pace.
    p. cm.
  Includes bibliographical references and index.
  ISBN 0-87579-411-4
    1. Christian leadership—Mormon Church.   2. Mormon Church—
Membership.   3. Church of Jesus Christ of Latter-day Saints—
Membership   I. Pace, R. Wayne.   II. Title.
BX8643.L4S74   1990
253—dc20   90-41857
                                                                CIP

Printed in the United States of America

10   9   8   7   6   5   4   3   2   1

To our splendid wives,
Sandra Utley Stephan and Gae Tueller Pace,
and a bunch of remarkable children

CONTENTS

ACKNOWLEDGMENTS

To all of those who have urged us to write about leadership, we express our immense gratitude. We want you to know that we approached this task with considerable fear and trembling, yet with excitement about the opportunity to think in new ways and to walk over previously uncharted ground to find a more effective approach to successful leadership. We have been awed, inspired, and instructed as we examined the life of the Savior as a perfect model of correct principles of leadership. We have been changed by this experience, and we now teach and counsel in new ways.

As we accept full responsibility for this writing, we gratefully recognize the valuable suggestions of those who reviewed the manuscript, especially Judy Smith and Don Norton. Through these pages we share our personal testimony of Jesus Christ—that he lives and invites all to "come unto me," "learn of me," "follow me."

A WORD BEFORE

Some of life's greatest personal calamities are caused by small leadership crises in a family, business, or community organization. All too often leaders compound their problems because they lack Christlike perspectives and fail to operate according to gospel principles.

Leadership acts touch upon so many aspects of our daily lives that the leadership process often eludes direct and accurate analysis. Both layman and scholar alike question the nature of that elusive process. Why do certain individuals attract such loyal followers? Can leaders be efficient without using raw power and authority? Is it possible to use the same principles of leadership at home as in the workplace? And which leadership style is the most effective?

Leadership is attributed to many different causes: kingly bloodlines, personality traits, specific actions, impelling circumstances that raise people to the occasion, and various combinations of all of these. We have been concerned with the scholarly study of leadership for more than thirty years. We have read, researched, and written about leadership. We have discussed, analyzed, and dissected the subject with friends, students, colleagues, and relatives. We have pon-

1

dered the topic in church meetings, in university classrooms, and in the hallways and walkways of hotels, cities, libraries, and offices.

We knew that effective leaders were, above everything else, men and women of action who attract followers to a cause or an idea. Leaders sense problems and initiate actions to resolve them. Yet every book we read failed to capture the excitement of such a simple idea. We were searching for the principles that produce that kind of delightful leadership, but we were confronted mostly with lists and discussions of abstract concepts and uninspiring techniques.

When we turned to the scriptures, we found what we had been fruitlessly searching for: the simple, essential principles that produce real leadership. We found treasures of knowledge in reading and pondering the scriptural accounts of the ways Jesus led people and raised them to their highest potential. From those accounts, we sought to construct a picture of the perfect leader.

Christlike Leadership

The life of Christ shows clearly that leadership, in its finest form, is much more than telling people what to do — a means of imposing one's will upon others. Jesus Christ is considered by Christians to be the greatest leader ever to walk the earth. For the master leader, perfect leadership is characterized by a willingness to serve rather than to be served. Jesus did not emphasize the authority of a ruler-leader but the humility of a servant-leader.

Jesus said many times, "Come, follow me," and continued to explain: "I am among you as he that serveth" (Luke 22:27). His approach to leadership emphasized "do what I do" rather than "do what I say." He walked and worked among his followers, listening to their needs,

2

responding to them lovingly, and making no harsh demands on others to satisfy his own desires.

In the Doctrine and Covenants the Lord warns: "We have learned by sad experience that it is the nature and disposition of almost all men, as soon as they get a little authority, as they suppose, they will immediately begin to exercise unrighteous dominion. Hence many are called, but few are chosen. No power or influence can or ought to be maintained by virtue of the priesthood, only by persuasion, by long-suffering, by gentleness and meekness, and by love unfeigned; by kindness, and pure knowledge, which shall greatly enlarge the soul without hypocrisy, and without guile" (D&C 121:39–42).

Avoiding unrighteous dominion and following the Savior's leadership example is not easy to do, but it can be done. President N. Eldon Tanner, a great church and business leader, suggested that "in order to lead as Jesus led, we are faced with many challenges. One of the first steps in meeting these challenges is to realize that Christ is a model of correct leadership; and, as the scriptures record his life and teachings, they become case studies of divine leadership" ("The Message," *New Era*, June 1977, p. 4). As we consider the scriptures and their case studies, the most dominant features of Christ's leadership become evident in his efforts to influence and direct his followers.

Emulate His Attributes

President Spencer W. Kimball explained to a group of potentially great leaders: "I make no apology for giving something of the accomplishments of Jesus Christ to those who seek success as leaders. If we would be eminently successful, here is our pattern. All the enobling, perfect, and beautiful qualities of maturity, of strength, and of courage are found

3

in this one person" ("Jesus: The Perfect Leader," *Ensign*, Aug. 1979, p. 5).

A thorough reading of Christ's daily activities as recorded in the Gospels shows Jesus as a man who was creative, persistent, confident, and of "good cheer." He enjoyed mingling with people and children. He loved crowds, and yet he found quiet moments when he could be alone.

He never panicked. There are no scriptural accounts of Jesus living his life in quiet desperation or perpetual sadness. He was filled with light, truth, and joy. Truly, he is the Great Exemplar, worthy to be emulated in every way. It is a most comforting thought to believe that we are a little like the Savior and that he is a little like us.

The attributes Jesus possessed and the principles he used to encourage his followers to action are the keys to perfect leadership. Those essential keys exemplified in the life of Christ help us learn to lead as the Savior led.

Five simple yet powerful leadership keys are elaborated upon in the following pages. That these keys are specific and quite easily understood encourages some of us who may dislike being formally appointed to positions of leadership or who might be a little intimidated by the problems associated with being the leader. The same fundamental keys give guidance to those who are called to be leaders or who want to help others become good leaders. Most of all, these correct and enduring keys of perfect leadership give yet another testimony of the divinity of Jesus Christ.

Our challenge as individuals is to look to the Savior and to continue to assimilate into our own lives the attributes and activities that characterize his perfect example of leadership. Today, the world is desperately in need of selfless, Christlike leadership. The rapid growth of the Church requires faithful men and women to assume leadership roles at every level. Exemplary leadership in business, industry, and government is sought after and generously rewarded. Families need to be unified and young people strengthened against unscrupulous enticements. Thus Christlike leadership in the home is absolutely essential. President David O. McKay described what can happen when we look to the Savior to meet such a challenge: "What you sincerely think in your heart of Christ will determine what you are, will largely determine what your acts will be. No person can study his divine personality, can accept his teachings, or follow his example, without becoming conscious of an uplifting and refining influence within himself" (*Man May Know for Himself*, p. 411).

We are quite confident that the question "Which of all the leadership theories most closely resembles the way in which Christ led others?" can be answered with unequivocal certainty, "None of them!" The thousands of different theories, skills, and attitudes that are described as vital for becoming a better leader can all be synthesized into one man: Jesus Christ.

Knowing now where to look for the correct approach to successful leadership, we can go forward together to examine the life of Christ as a demonstration of five quintessential keys to effective leadership. Perhaps we will glimpse the extraordinary adventure of perfect leadership and its challenge for all of us. "We can see and understand only a little about God now, as if we were peering at His reflection in a poor mirror: but someday we are going to see Him in His completeness, face to face" (*Reach Out*, p. 422).

1

THE FIRST KEY:
TREAT OTHERS AS FRIENDS

Supper ended.

The disciples shifted to find comfortable places.

Jesus rose, poured water into a basin, and began to wash the disciples' feet.

When he had finished, he sat down and asked, "Know ye what I have done to you? Ye call me Master and Lord. . . . If I then, your Lord and Master, have washed your feet; ye also ought to wash one another's feet. For I have given you an example, that ye should do as I have done to you" (John 13:12–15).

Then Christ gave his disciples the key to understanding the relationship that should exist between leaders and their followers: "Henceforth I call you not servants; for the servant knoweth not what his lord doeth: but I have called you friends; for all things that I have heard of my Father I have made known unto you" (John 15:15).

Great leaders try to replace the master/servant and superior/subordinate relationship with a more trusting, friend-to-friend association. If Christ is to be our leader, we must be his friend. If we are his friends, we will follow him. In modern scripture, Christ explains that "it is expedient that I give unto you this commandment, that ye become even as my friends in days when I was with them" (D&C 84:77).

If we want to follow him, we must become his friends. To become a friend is to become an ally, to unite and join together for a specific purpose. The penetrating question, then, is how Christ, beyond giving a commandment, encouraged followers and strangers to become his friends.

Christ's leadership style is intimately interwoven with his admonition to become a friend. The first quintessential key to Christlike leadership is to treat others as friends.

What Is a Friend?

Synonyms for the word *friend* chart the landscape of the territory of being a friend. A friend is an acquaintance, a comrade, a companion, a chum, a confidant, a partner, a buddy, a pal, a sidekick, a crony, a cohort, and a consort. A friend is also a patron, supporter, backer, benefactor, a well-wisher, an encourager, an advocate, a defender, a partisan, and an adherent. In addition, friends are as allies, colleagues, associates, brothers, and followers.

The word *friendship* and its synonyms sketch the features that characterize a friend. For example, friendship means having a good feeling toward another, harmony, accord, amicableness, consonance, understanding, sympathy, good fellowship, cordiality, neighborliness, and goodwill.

A friendly person is one who is kindly, helpful, well-disposed, amiable, neighborly, amicable, loving, familiar, affectionate, kindhearted, cordial, genial, warmhearted, ardent, devoted, sympathetic, gracious, generous, chummy, companionable, convivial, hospitable, social, accessible, and affable.

Leadership as the creation of friends is such a profound

concept that it turns ordinary definitions of leadership on their heads.

We usually think of leadership as influencing others through interpersonal communication. We usually think of the leader as the most influential person in the group. The idea of leading people connotes that someone is out in front and others are behind. Great leaders are those who take charge, who motivate people, who set goals and direct people toward them. Many associate the concept of leadership with people who boss, command, guide, blaze trails, wheel, deal, and seize the reins.

The popular concept of leading implies being the head, supreme, great, preeminent, unrivaled, unparalleled, stellar, and topmost. Slang words indicate how some people think about a leader: bigwig, kingpin, magnate, mogul, tycoon, and godfather.

A dramatic contrast is evident between the meaning of *friend* and the popular meaning of *leader*. Friends have a long and abiding mature love for one another. They sacrifice for one another; they do for one another what each would do for the other. One is not superior nor the other subordinate; one is not leader while the other follows; they are true and authentic brothers and sisters, equal in each other's sight. Friends are generous and hospitable with one another. They are devoted and genial, happy to be in the presence of each other. They are willing to place the needs of the other ahead of their own.

One of the greatest stories of friendship ever recorded is that of Damon and Pythias. Pythias was thrown into prison for an offense against the king. Because Pythias was married and had a family, Damon offered to take his place in prison while Pythias went home to say good-bye to his family. The king was so impressed by the offer that he agreed to the

9

arrangement, provided Damon were to suffer death in Pythias' place if Pythias failed to return. Damon accepted the plan.

At the appointed hour, Pythias had not arrived and Damon was taken to the place of execution. Moments before Damon was to be put to death, Pythias returned and took his place. The king was so amazed that Pythias would keep his promise to Damon, even though keeping his promise meant losing his life, that the king released them both.

The total commitment of Damon and Pythias to one another is characteristic of true friendship. These friends symbolize in an earthly way the heavenly and divine friendship of Christ with his disciples and the members of his Church. Complete and total willingness to accept the burdens of others is the fulness of friendship, toward which we strive when we follow Christ's example of leadership.

A Friend-to-Friend Bond

Leadership is a friend-to-friend bond warranted by a resolute determination to fulfill a sacred vow. Leadership as that friend-to-friend bond is the challenge we are seeking to meet. When a friend-to-friend relationship elicits a pledge, resolution, and decision to stand for others, to serve them, and to raise them in stature and character, that bond illustrates the kind of leadership exemplified by the Perfect Leader. To hear Christ say that we are his friends is a thrilling and strengthening experience. To feel and know that someone loves us, believes in us, trusts us, and expects good things from us is inspiring. Pure, powerful, loving friendship binds people to one another.

The challenge of perfect leadership is to cultivate strong friendships. People follow those whom they like; they like their friends and go along with them. Friendship creates a willingness to follow. Christ loves us; he is our friend. We love Christ; we are his friends. We are willing to follow him.

Friendship establishes the foundation upon which leadership can be exercised. You cannot lead an enemy. You can lead friends. Friendship makes leadership more effective and much easier to achieve. It is easier to invite friends to be involved. It is easier to want to serve a friend. It is easier to be committed to a friend. We accept encouragement more easily by friends.

The very nature of friendship—as a feeling of loving, helpful, kind, and dedicated associates—fulfills the deep longing all of us have for someone with whom we can share and grow. "Among life's sweetest blessings," said David O. McKay, "is fellowship with men and women whose ideals and aspirations are high and noble. Next to a sense of kinship with God come the helpfulness, encouragement, and inspiration of friends. Friendship is a sacred possession. . . . 'To live, laugh, love one's friends, and be loved by them is to bask in the sunshine of life' " (*Gospel Ideals*, p. 253).

Joseph Smith stated that friendship is one of the "grand fundamental principles of Mormonism." He said further, "Friendship is like Brother Turley in his blacksmith shop welding iron to iron; it unites the human family with its happy influence" (*Teachings of the Prophet Joseph Smith*, p. 316).

You can be a leader without being or having a friend, but you will have chosen the more difficult route. Being a friend is the simpler, easier, more effective way to achieve Christlike leadership. Being a friend opens the door to exciting, moving, powerful leadership, without the use of complex, lengthy strategies for winning and influencing people. By being a friend and having a friend, you have the basis for great leadership.

Friendship is both universal and imperative for leadership because it applies to the temporal and the spiritual aspects of leading. Friendship is the basis of Christ's effective leadership. It can also be the basis of our own effective leadership. That does not mean that we can avoid all other approaches to leadership, but leadership techniques are markedly less effective when we are not working with friends. Leadership methods are much more effective when we work with friends. The number and complexity of leadership techniques can be measurably reduced when we begin with the assumption of friendship.

A father of seven beautiful children announced during a sacrament meeting talk that he had been a father for thirty-five years and did not want to be a parent anymore. He explained that he had observed how wonderfully his children treated their friends. He noticed that they spent hours on the phone talking together. They dreamed together and defended each other and enjoyed being with each other for long periods of time. The father said that he would rather be treated as a friend than as a parent. Serious faces turned into smiles as the audience began to chuckle and nod their approval of the idea.

The father, feeling that he was getting his point across, then looked directly at his wife and announced that he did not want to be a husband anymore. Briefly he recounted their several years of exciting courtship. Apparently they had spent much time together talking about the future, present, and past. Together they learned how to dance and play tennis. They were proud of each other, defended each other, and spoke frequently on the telephone. Above all, he said, "I treated my sweetheart as my best friend. She was my best friend. And I believe that I would rather be her best friend again."

12

Maybe he was trying to explain that friendship precedes great fatherhood and great motherhood or maybe that in marriage, romance may decrease but friendship lasts forever. Friendship also precedes great leadership.

Other leadership theories, based on the assumption that people are not and can never be friends, provide weaker, more complex methods for leading. In front of a crackling fire in Vail, Colorado, a small group of successful business leaders considered the subject of executive leadership. One executive introduced the idea that it might be possible to lead with love and to be friends with employees and even competitors. A hearty laugh filled the room, and a rush of comments quickly followed. "Are you kidding?" one person shouted out. "You would immediately be labeled a pushover and a soft negotiator. You'd be annihilated and probably bankrupt in less than six months." Others agreed.

The thought that leading others can be made more effective and easier by operating on the fundamental principle of friendship was discussed no further that evening. It almost seemed as though the rough and tough approach to leadership had won out. Yet, strangely, everyone in the room was trying to be friendly to each other.

Friendship built on a true concern for the other person is not a soft acquiescence to problems or to mediocre performance. On the contrary, a good friend tells a close companion in need, "I understand," not "I agree with what you are doing or the way you are handling the situation." A friend does not spend much time wallowing in self-pity but asks, "What can we do to improve the situation?" The consummate relationship we must have if we are to exercise divine leadership effectively is friend to friend. Thus the first quintessential key to Christlike leadership is to treat others as friends.

Love

What general attitude underlies a radiant friend-to-friend relationship? The answer is simple and is available to all of us. Genuine friendship, like that in a Christlike relationship, is fired, fueled, driven, motivated, and made real by love. In both ancient and modern scripture we read the clear call to follow by reason of love: "If ye love me, keep my commandments" (John 14:15) and "If thou lovest me thou shalt serve me and keep all my commandments" (D&C 42:29).

Love forms a strong bond and is dispensed unceasingly by Jesus Christ and our Eternal Father. The prophet Nephi wrote that the most desirable thing we could receive from God "is the love of God, which sheddeth itself abroad in the hearts of the children of men; wherefore, it is the most desirable above all things. . . . and the most joyous to the soul" (1 Nephi 11:21–23).

Love binds people to each other and unites them with God. All things are easier to do when they are done for someone we love and respect. Because we love and admire Christ, we are able to follow him. Obligations are easier to keep and goals easier to achieve when they are sought in love.

Jesus demonstrated unabashed love toward his disciples when he washed their feet at the Last Supper. No thought of impropriety or humiliation entered his mind as he knelt before each apostle.

Peter, however, was startled. To witness a divine person humble himself by washing the dust from the feet of his followers and toweling them dry created an unforgettable memory. Even more astonishing to Peter was the later realization that Jesus did not hesitate to wash the feet of Judas, who was in the very process of betraying Christ. No doubt

14

the apostles learned that to be Christlike, the line between master and servant must be obliterated. All must be served — the leper, the orphan, the widow, the elderly, the poor, the misguided.

After the washing, the conversation focused on the love of the apostles for one another. Jesus spoke intimately but confidently. He concluded his final discourse with the most significant admonitions of his sacred ministry: "Little children, yet a little while I am with you. . . . A new commandment I give unto you, That ye love one another; as I have loved you, that ye also love one another. By this shall all men know that ye are my disciples, if ye have love one to another" (John 13:33–35). Jesus' demonstration of humility and love by washing the feet of his disciples was now followed by the admonition to love one another, even as Jesus loved them.

These last urgings of Christ are significant because he did not intend them only for the apostles but for all of us (John 17:20–21). They remind us that love grows out of friendship.

Create a friend-to-friend relationship, and you also create the basis for true love. Out of friendship grows Christlike love. Perfect leadership begins when we treat others as friends.

2

THE SECOND KEY: CREATE A POSITIVE FORCE

The story of Jesus is of a young boy growing up in a humble family, increasing in his abilities to teach and lead others, suffering disappointments and sorrow, and building such a strong following that his influence was only beginning to be felt at the time of his death. Christ's magnificent life and legacy are the greatest leadership model and success story of all time.

Jesus, like most of us, did not start at the top of a well-developed organization, nor did he have wealthy and influential parents to assure him a position of power and influence in his community. He grew up in Nazareth, a small town some distance from Jerusalem. Even when reports spread that a prophet-leader had arisen from that country town, the question was asked, with an air of derision, "Can there any good thing come out of Nazareth?" (John 1:46).

Good things and good people, nevertheless, did come out of Nazareth. In fact, Jesus of Nazareth has affected the lives of millions of people for thousands of years. His powerful leadership attributes melded to produce a dynamic force that influenced his followers to act. His energetic and incisive leadership style was characterized by three central features: a strong commitment to the task at hand, a great compassion for the people he led, and a consistently encouraging attitude. By reading about the life of Christ in the scriptures, we can learn to magnify those three attributes in ourselves. They constitute an inner force that is, indeed, the very soul of true leadership.

Leading with Commitment

Early in his ministry, Jesus had an opportunity to confirm his commitment to his leadership role. The scriptures record that after being in the wilderness for forty days without eating, Jesus was tempted three times by Satan, who said, "If thou be the Son of God, command this stone that it be made bread" (Luke 4:3). Satan first challenged Jesus to use his power to satisfy physical and material needs — to put temporal things ahead of spiritual things. He could satisfy his hunger immediately and then continue to achieve considerable material gain by abandoning his divine purpose and his earthly ministry. He could use his inherent power for selfish reasons rather than service to others.

For the second temptation, Luke reports, Satan took Jesus up onto a high mountain, showed him all the kingdoms of the world, and said to him: "All this power will I give thee, and the glory of them: for that is delivered unto me; and to whomsoever I will I give it" (Luke 4:6). Jesus could have earthly splendor, power, and glory. He could give up his messianic mission and gather considerable fame and fortune for himself.

In a third effort, Satan tempted Jesus to verify his status as the Son of God. Satan "set him on a pinnacle of the temple" and challenged Jesus to cast himself down from the pinnacle of the temple so that angels would bear him up, "lest at any time thou dash thy foot against a stone" (Luke 4:11).

We are not certain whether Jesus was literally placed upon a high pinnacle of the temple or not, but we do know that temptation is a point of decision. We know that temptation tests us and requires us to make a choice. We also know that temptations come directly from Satan and indirectly from our own flesh and the world around us. It is natural to desire recognition and reward for what we do. Sometimes, however, rewards are promised to us only if we agree to certain conditions. A young woman may be asked to permit sexual liberties in return for a young man's undying devotion. A young man may be promised great monetary rewards if he deals in drugs. A businessman may be promised success if he engages in questionable or dishonest transactions. Each of us must examine our choices to see if what we are sacrificing is really worth it. There is no question that temptations are real. If we resist them and overcome them, we prove our worthiness to be friends and companions with Jesus Christ.

The record of the Savior's experiences with temptation gives us a pattern to follow when we experience our own moments of concern, as when doubts enter our minds about accepting a position of leadership and responsibility. Recently a faithful young mother was called to an important leadership responsibility in her stake. The anticipation of becoming acquainted with a new program and trying to lead people with whom she wasn't particularly well acquainted was almost overwhelming. To make matters worse, she was a single parent trying to raise a family, work, and go to school. You can imagine the struggle in her mind as she considered what might be gained by accepting the calling in contrast to what might be achieved at work or in school

19

if she rejected the position. She could devote all her time to other important aspects of her life. This devoted young woman nevertheless followed the humble man from Galilee into the wilderness and received confirmation through prayer to accept the calling. Both Jesus and this woman were real people, in real places, reaching for the vision, the power, and the confidence that are the very heart and soul of leadership.

Having been taught by the Spirit and having received the assurance of his divine mission, Jesus put Satan's temptations behind him. Hence, he came away strengthened and fully committed. The scriptures record, "Jesus returned in the power of the Spirit into Galilee: and there went out a fame of him through all the region round about" (Luke 4:14).

His commitment became visible through his cause. All leaders commit themselves to a cause, but that is not enough. True leaders commit themselves to a good cause, a purpose beyond the everyday activities of daily living. Great leaders are committed to great causes that become the focus of their constant and patient devotion.

If we ever dream of becoming great at anything, we might begin by asking ourselves, "Am I going to allow daily activities to govern my life, or am I going to live my life according to noble principles?" Unless we consciously decide to do more than engage in the routine necessities of daily living, our lives will inevitably become shallow. Though Jesus still had much growing to do, accompanied by further temptations (see Luke 22:28), he clearly knew his purpose.

Unlike some of us who are at times uncertain whether we are using our time and energy appropriately, Jesus acted and spoke with great authority, sincerity, and courage, magnifying his calling at every opportunity. Imagine how startled Nicodemus must have been when Jesus boldly declared to that important man, a member of the Sanhedrin, "Verily, verily, I say unto thee, Except a man be born again, he cannot see the kingdom of God" (John 3:3). Remember the rich man's surprise when Jesus advised him to sell all that he had and distribute it to the poor, so that he would have treasures in heaven, and then to come without hesitation and faithfully follow him (see Matthew 19:16–22).

Jesus' cause was clear, and he pressed forward with daring ideas and powerful language. Consider further the courage and determination he derived from his commitment when he cleansed the temple of money changers and how he answered the Pharisees' challenge to his authority. Recall that the Pharisees prided themselves on their strict observance of the law and their overzealous belief in both written and oral religious tradition. Jesus had just declared, "I am the light of the world: he that followeth me shall not walk in darkness, but shall have the light of life." Almost lightning quick, the Pharisees responded, "Thou bearest record of thyself; thy record is not true." Without hesitation, Jesus replied, "Though I bear record of myself, yet my record is true: for I *know* whence I came, and whither I go" (John 8:12–14; emphasis added).

When called to a leadership position, we too can "study it out" in our minds and pray about it (D&C 9:8). We can also alleviate some of our concerns by talking to someone who holds or has held a similar position. By asking for their help in learning how to perform more effectively in the new calling, we can benefit. Quite often a new bishop or Relief Society president will sit down with the former counterpart and ask for information and advice. New parents frequently turn to their own parents for encouragement and direction.

Wise leaders study, pray, and seek sound advice to alleviate their anxieties and confirm their commitment to serve and lead.

After we have followed the Savior's example, wrestled with various considerations, and received the assurance that we can succeed in our leadership position, we then must perform well and accomplish much. A leader who accepts a position without being committed to achieve appropriate goals simply blocks the path for others who want to serve and assist. If a home teacher, for example, is not making regular visits to a family or if those visits are perfunctory and do not attend to the real needs of the family, then that home teacher blocks the way for someone else to better serve the family.

The same problem exists in business. There is a management saying that goes like this: Reward or replace. When someone is not doing well in a position and does not want to learn how to do the job better, the only alternative is to replace the person. It is not just a matter of replacing an uncommitted individual or taking the time and money to train someone else. The main goal is to get the work done.

All leadership positions, whether in the family, church, or workplace, give us opportunities for personal growth and development as well as provide us with more ways to render service. Leadership opportunities also allow us to discover how the organization functions. And the rewards for committed leadership invariably multiply, whether we want them to or not.

A recent graduate of a university in New York took a job with one of America's largest banking corporations. She was asked to write executive memos and prepare articles for the employees' magazine. She decided that even though she wasn't in the most enviable job, she would do her very best.

She quickly learned about the banking business and the organizational structure of the huge banking conglomerate by conducting interviews to get information for the articles and memos. She learned that customer service was the driving force of the banking industry, and she set a marvelous example of quality work for her co-workers. She won an award for producing the best in-house publication for banking employees. When her supervisor saw the results of her intense loyalty and commitment to the company, she was promoted to a position of greater responsibility.

Leading with Compassion

Jesus' boldness and directness in leading people to the truth of the gospel were always tempered by his genuine concern for their feelings and needs. When the scribes and Pharisees brought an adulterous woman to Jesus, they confidently declared that the law of Moses required that such a woman be stoned. "But what sayest thou?" they taunted. Jesus showed his compassion by first ridding the woman of her accusers. He said to them, "He that is without sin among you, let him first cast a stone at her." When the scribes and Pharisees, "being convicted by their own conscience," went away, Jesus then lovingly advised the woman, "Neither do I condemn thee: go, and sin no more" (John 8:5–11).

This whole incident suggests that we first put our own lives in order and then learn to deal more compassionately with others. Jesus not only startled those pious, "better than thou," would-be stone-throwers by asking them to look inside themselves but demonstrated how to be compassionate and understanding to someone who had stumbled and erred along the way. The brevity of his response is priceless: "Neither do I condemn thee: go, and sin no more."

Because we all make mistakes, it is easy to be critical

23

and judgmental of each other. Two professional basketball officials were sitting in a hot steam room discussing their different approaches to refereeing. Apparently the younger official had been to refresher seminars and was acquainted with new rule changes and interpretations. During the discussion, questions were raised about when contact fouls should be called, when moving screens should be penalized, and when a variety of other rule violations should be recognized. The younger referee overanxiously displayed his seemingly infinite knowledge of the rules. The older referee then said something that quite surprised his younger colleague: "If I called a rule infraction every time I was aware of one, I would be stopping the game every three to five seconds. The goal of refereeing is having a fair game, not calling fouls."

Many of our mistakes are so trivial that they are not worth dwelling on. Those that are significant should be handled with great compassion and dispatched as quickly as possible. We fail to show compassion when we use tactless and offensive ways of saying things. Such verbal abuse must be guarded against every hour of the day if we want to develop Christlike attributes of leadership and truly lead with compassion.

Someone has said that our mouths get us into more trouble than any other part of us. Proverbs advises, "Whoso keepeth his mouth and his tongue keepeth his soul from troubles" (Proverbs 21:23). In Psalms David pleads with the Lord to "set a watch, O Lord, before my mouth; keep the door of my lips" (Psalms 141:3). James gives us some excellent advice about communicating with each other: "Let every man be swift to hear, slow to speak, and slow to wrath" (James 1:19). A few verses after that admonition to listen more than we speak and to control our emotions, James says, "If any man among you seem to be religious, and bridleth not his tongue, but deceiveth in his own heart, this man's religion is vain" (James 1:26).

Often, especially when we are tired or in a hurry, we say things that threaten and undermine our relationships with others. For example, a church member had been asked to offer the opening prayer at a large gathering. The person conducting the meeting approached the brother to remind him of the request and to invite him to be seated on the stand. He blurted out, "Remember you're giving the opening prayer. Keep it brief. Take your seat." Then he quickly turned and walked away. The curtness of the directions and the coldness of the vocal expression created a lack of feeling for the occasion. In addition, the sudden detachment and abrupt departure undermined a potentially warm and positive relationship between the person conducting and the person asked to give the prayer.

Compassionate leaders should be concerned not only with the ways in which they communicate but also with the personal and physical needs of their followers. Jesus repeatedly demonstrated his great understanding and concern for the basic needs of his people. Mark records that on more than one occasion Jesus called his disciples to him and explained, "I have compassion on the multitude, because they have now been with me three days and have nothing to eat: and if I send them away fasting to their own houses, they will faint by the way" (Mark 8:2–3). At that time, the people really needed food to eat, and the Savior provided that food.

Adequate food, clothing, shelter, transportation, or health care are sometimes the unexpressed but real needs of our friends and co-workers. A personal relationship may have gone awry and greatly affected the ability of a follower

25

to perform his or her work. Inadequate resources to do an assignment or the lack of an appropriate place to work may be major deterrents to excellent performance.

A single parent in a ward, who had finally adjusted to life without a husband, needed something more than friendly advice and encouragement. Her car wasn't operating properly, the water taps in her apartment were leaking, the oven needed electrical work to stabilize the cooking temperature, and the children's bikes were broken. Fortunately, a home teacher and an elder's quorum president were creative and sensitive enough to recognize some practical needs of this struggling young mother. They took steps to fix the car, replace faucet washers, repair the oven, and arrange for a couple of used bicycles to be given to the children.

Leading with compassion requires a great understanding of the needs of followers as well as a strong commitment to helping and healing wherever possible. Jesus' personal influence and power with his followers came from his deep, sympathetic understanding of their needs, and his constant and patient efforts to respond appropriately.

Leading with Encouragement

The simplest way to encourage others is to recognize their talent and potential. Jesus pleads with us to believe in ourselves: "Ye are the salt of the earth" and "the light of the world. . . Let your light so shine before men, that they may see your good works, and glorify your Father which is in heaven" (Matthew 5:13–14, 16).

He outlined our greatest potential and possibilities in his simple declaration: "Be ye therefore perfect, even as your Father which is in heaven is perfect" (Matthew 5:48). We can lead in the same manner, giving encouragement and lifting our associates with words and actions that suggest they have unlimited potential.

A famous university football coach, with one of the best winning records, does everything in his power to get his football players to believe in themselves. He teaches them the fundamentals of the game: blocking, tackling, and teamwork. Then he encourages each player to perform to the best of his ability. He does not dwell on the players' faults or their weaknesses but focuses on their strengths. Each year the team's objective is to play in a major bowl game. In practice, the players see how committed the coach is to achieving the goal and how totally committed he is to them. They in turn respond by doing things on the playing field that other coaches say border on the supernatural. Accordingly, they perform well enough to receive an invitation each year to play in a college bowl game.

A sage once said, "The best way to change people is to treat them as if they had already changed." In other words, respecting a person's talents and potential encourages positive change.

When the pathway to a better way of life became rough and difficult for Jesus' followers, he lifted their heads and hearts by substituting understanding for fear and cheerfulness for a sad countenance. "Be of good cheer" became one of Christ's more familiar phrases. In healing a man stricken with palsy, Jesus encouraged him to "be of good cheer; thy sins be forgiven thee" (Matthew 9:2). Nearer the end of his life, Jesus explained to his disciples that they would be scattered, "every man to his own," and that "in the world ye shall have tribulation: but be of good cheer; I have overcome the world" (John 16:32–33).

When Paul the Apostle went from city to city, trying to preach the gospel, his life was often threatened, and he faced

27

all kinds of tribulations. After one particularly difficult day, the scriptures witness: "And the night following the Lord stood by him, and said, Be of good cheer, Paul: For as thou hast testified of me in Jerusalem, so must thou bear witness also at Rome" (Acts 23:11).

We can smile a little as we imagine the Lord saying, "Be of good cheer. I know that you got beat up a little today. But wait until you see what's in store for you over there in Rome tomorrow!" On the other hand, we can also comprehend the encouragement that comes from someone whom we admire, filled with enlightment, peace, and power, who visits us when we are sick and discouraged and says, "Be of good cheer. It is I, your neighbor. Do not be afraid. I can help." If we are true followers of Christ, we can go to our families, friends, and work associates with the same healing influence. We can say, with great love and confidence, "Don't worry. I am here. Everything is going to be all right now."

Happiness is not an external condition. It is an attitude and a state of mind. Though we may be influenced by conditions and events that surround us, we have final control over whether we are happy or sad. Sometimes we forget that Christ and his apostles faced dreary, rainy, wintry days in Jerusalem. The weather was not always sunny and pleasant. They also had to deal with unscrupulous officials in the local government and crafty spokesmen of various religious groups. Life was not easy. Had Jesus based his happiness on others or on the weather, he would have been riding an emotional roller coaster for most of his life.

Because happiness is an attitude, we can control our own state of being. A university professor was sitting in his office with a big grin on his face. A colleague of his walked

28

past the open door, noticed the smile, and inquired, "What's wrong?"

"Nothing," replied the still grinning professor.

The inquirer then commented on all the problems the department was facing and concluded that these were difficult times and many people were unhappy. "How can you be smiling at a time like this?" he asked.

The reply was utterly simple and startling. "I choose to be happy."

The professor was not ignorant of the inequities and the administrative problems around him, and he was trying to correct some obvious wrongs. Nevertheless, he refused to let his happiness fluctuate because of someone else's unhappiness or sad circumstances.

Jesus encouraged his followers to be of good cheer. He constantly tried to gladden their hearts and raise their spirits. In the Sermon on the Mount, for example, Christ specifically taught nine beatitudes, or ways to receive comfort and happiness. Each beatitude begins with the word *blessed.* To be blessed means to be happy, fortunate, and content. If we want constant, inner happiness, we can choose to live the spiritual rules for happiness. Jesus himself shared happiness because he had inner contentment—he lived the Beatitudes before he taught them.

To follow Christ's example is to go against the things that the world portrays as leading to happiness. Glamorized all around us are the actions of swearing, adultery, and violence. Nevertheless, Jesus condemned not only these actions but also the very thoughts that precipitate the acts. Control the thought, and you control the act (Matthew 5 and 6).

In the Sermon on the Mount Jesus attempted to help us look inward. If we actively examine our own thoughts and attitudes, we can then exercise control over how we feel. If we choose to be happy during the day and replace discouragement and gloom with hope and joy, we begin to free our own hearts. At the same time we need to encourage others to do the same. Like the Savior, we can lie down at night knowing we tried our best not to offend or discourage anyone. Our conscience is clear.

Everyone Can Lead

All of us, men and women alike, with all our human imperfections and limitations, can succeed in leadership opportunities by seeking the same attributes of commitment, compassion, and cheerfulness that characterized Christ's remarkable leadership style. Belle S. Spafford reminds us that the Master saw beyond the initial weaknesses and frailties of the original Twelve Apostles to their greater strengths and leadership potential: "How well these men succeeded in their callings is borne out by scripture. Peter, despite his impulsive nature, grew to such stature as to become the head of Christ's earthly organization. Matthew, a hated publican, has given to the world a record of Christ's ministry that has directed the lives of millions. John, referred to as a son of thunder because of the force of his wrath, is today universally accepted as 'John, the beloved' " (*Women in Today's World*, p. 66).

Everyone has the potential to become a Christlike leader by developing a positive force that inspires those who follow them. Christ was fully committed to his work, consummately compassionate toward people, and consistently encouraging in the face of adversity. The Savior's invitation is extended to each of us: "Therefore, what manner of men ought ye to be? Verily I say unto you, even as I am" (3 Nephi 27:27).

30

3

THE THIRD KEY:
INVITE OTHERS TO FOLLOW

Christ came not only to redeem the world but also to establish his kingdom. The perfect leader, Jesus treated people as friends and showed commitment, compassion, and encouragement—all essential parts of leadership. At the same time, he provided direction toward a meaningful and significant goal. He organized a strong following of people who carried on the work of administering the saving principles and ordinances of the gospel.

After being tempted by Satan in the wilderness, Jesus returned to his hometown of Nazareth and "went into the synagogue on the sabbath day, and stood up for to read" (Luke 4:16). Picture Jesus entering the synagogue to read from the scriptures. From the book of Esaias, he read the phrase "The Spirit of the Lord is upon me, because he hath anointed me to preach the gospel to the poor" and closed the book. He then sat down, the eyes of the entire congregation on him. He added, "This day is this scripture fulfilled in your ears" (Luke 4:17–21).

The gripping events that often engulf a bold and courageous leader followed. The people seized Jesus, dragged him to the outskirts of the city to the brow of a hill to throw him over the cliff. That dramatic act did not conclude as they expected, however: "but he passing through the midst of them went his way" (Luke 4:30). Unaffected by the ire of the unruly crowd, Jesus took command of the situation and calmly walked through the mob in complete control.

Jesus did not hesitate to take the lead and invite people to follow him. Here is a person with powerful leadership abilities; a person with purpose, direction, and goals. He is a leader whom we can and should follow. In fact, Christ invited us to follow him when he said, "Come, follow me" (Luke 18:22).

The simplest phrases often convey the most powerful meanings to the human mind. Such is the case with the utterance "Come, follow me." The essence of leadership is expressed in these words. To lead is to go before or show the way; guide the direction, course, action, or opinion. To lead is often thought of as being out in front, or proceeding first.

The phrase "Come, follow me" perfectly characterizes the primary act of leadership. The leader goes before and requests others to follow. Jesus did not wait for others — he led the way. Although that may seem elementary, the life of Jesus demonstrates that he constantly took the first step and invited others to follow. The scriptures are filled with incidents in which Jesus led the way.

A simple instance occurred a few days after the feeding of the five thousand people with five loaves and two fishes. Luke records, "He took Peter and John and James, and went up into a mountain to pray" (Luke 9:28). The great leader may have said, "Come, follow me" and led them to the mountain. He did not say, "Go up there. I'll meet you later." Christ led the way, and then he asked the disciples to follow him.

Leadership, as demonstrated by the perfect leader, consists of taking the initiative and firmly but patiently pleading with others to come and follow. Consider the feast of the dedication in Jerusalem. It was winter, and Jesus was walking in the temple in Solomon's porch. The Jews were divided over whether Jesus was a devil, a madman, or the Christ. A number of the Jews gathered around Jesus and asked, "How long dost thou make us to doubt? If thou be the Christ, tell us plainly." Jesus replied, "I told you, and ye believed not" (John 10:22–25).

Once again Jesus seized the inititative and led the way. He explained that he is the Good Shepherd: "I am the good shepherd, and know my sheep, and am known of mine." He said further that if they didn't believe him, then they should believe in "the works that I do in my Father's name, they bear witness of me. . . . I and my Father are one" (John 10: 14, 25, 30). Filled with resentment and rage, the Jews wanted to stone him. Jesus did not flinch. Bouyed up by knowing who he was and what his purpose was, his being was flooded with calmness and strength. Not a rock was thrown nor a hand laid upon him as he departed out of their presence.

Involving others as the Savior did requires having a visionary purpose, providing constant direction, speaking with conviction, and giving patient instruction.

Visionary Purpose

Jesus was driven forward by the vision of his earthly purpose. Even as a youth, he understood his great and wonderful calling. The incident in the temple, where his parents found him "sitting in the midst of the doctors, both hearing them, and asking them questions," illustrates his deep understanding. His reply to the anxious question of his mother,

33

"How is it that ye sought me? wist ye not that I must be about my Father's business?" clearly indicates his vision of his purpose (Luke 2:46, 49).

As leaders, we must also know what business we are about. We must have personal goals and a direction. A university student, who was also the owner and manager of a small business, wrote: "I desire with all my heart and in deep humility to be able to emulate the life of Jesus Christ, for he is indeed the perfect example of an effective leader. I intend to be industrious, compassionate, and encouraging in my endeavors to be a successful businessman, father, husband, and Latter-day Saint. Specifically, I hope to be a good listener, to create a vision, to involve others, and to show unconditional love to those with whom I come in contact. The values I hold dear will be supported and remain consistent as I display my commitment to these principles as a daily example to my family and associates."

We can clarify and develop our own goals if we begin with a sound understanding of the very purpose of life itself: to know that God lives, that we are his children, and that we are endowed with the potential to rise to the stature of God. That purpose inspires us to great personal effort to move from wherever we are toward perfection. Our purpose stimulates our individual development.

Setting personal goals also makes us more attractive leaders. Unless those around us see us striving for worthy achievements, they will not look to us as good examples to follow. They will quickly recognize that we are not committed to the tasks that need to be accomplished.

Leaders have the opportunity and obligation to envision future expectations for their organization. Leaders who have made a difference in major corporations around the world were visionary; they dared to dream dreams. They imagined

34

in their minds what could be, and invited others to follow by articulating the dream in a way that made it possible to achieve.

Motivation research and practice indicate that people look for something beyond the wages and benefits of a job to excite and energize them. Employees desire to be part of something bigger. They want to share in a group or organizational goal. For instance, some employees at a large aircraft facility spoke about *their* company and how *they* had just sent a missile into orbit. It sounded as if they owned the company and had personally fired the missile from the launch pad that was located more than two thousand miles from where they worked. They were excited because they were part of a big and wonderful accomplishment.

A leader foresees the end of a project and envisions possible outcomes. The question for the leader is "What do we want to have happen?" The answer to such a question is nearly always found in an image of the result, in a vision of the future. Consider any project or organization — a ward party, a quorum, or the ward Relief Society. What is the most critical asset the leader can have? The answer is a vision of what the party, the quorum, or the ward Relief Society could be like.

Effective leaders imagine the grand view of the very best. What should happen at the very best party? What should occur in the very best quorum or the very best Relief Society? Likewise, what expectations should be set for the very best family, or very best stake?

A newly organized ward Relief Society presidency held their first leadership meeting. The new president, a young, wise woman, described her dreams for the Relief Society to her counselors and secretary. She desired to have the sisters unite in a spirit of love for each other and be taught by the

Spirit of the Lord. She wanted them to be fortified and in-spired to render Christlike service to their families and neighbors. This Relief Society president felt that her coun-selors, who were key people in leading the other sisters, should have an opportunity to add to the vision. The first counselor commented that all should share the experience of being gathered together to receive enlightened instruction. Sisters who are unable to attend a meeting should be im-mediately contacted and the weekly message of inspiration should be shared with them so that they feel included and informed. "I see our sisters in constant contact with each other, strengthening and supporting each other outside of our Relief Society meetings. They network for increased motivation and to render compassionate service to one an-other," said the other counselor. Thus was born a vision for that particular ward Relief Society.

A vision may not be 100 percent practical or 100 percent achievable, but it must be exciting and stimulating. It must stir our imagination and cause us to reach. A mother and father can dream together about their perfect family. What should it be like, how should family members act, what should be achieved, what directions should they take? Bishops can create in their minds the great ward. Young Women leaders can find in their minds and hearts the best application of the Young Women's program for their girls. A deacons quorum president, with the help of an advisor, can envision the very best quorum meetings and projects.

Years ago, the vision of a great stake was grasped by a young stake president in a rural area. When the Church published a list of the leading stakes, he studied their names as he milked the cows. He wondered why certain stakes were listed. He met with the high council and asked them what a stake did to be listed as the number one stake in the

Church. The stake clerks gathered figures that showed the differences between their stake and the number one stake. He began to get a vision of where the stake should be going and what it should be doing.

At the next conference, the stake president vividly described his vision to the membership and counseled them to follow their leaders. The bishops, priesthood quorum leaders, Mutual presidencies, Sunday School presidencies, and Relief Society presidencies caught the vision. They all agreed to do what was necessary to make their stake the number one stake in the Church for the very next year. Attendance at meetings shot up, and ward activities increased. Priesthood quorums involved their members in every way possible in the rural communities within the stake boundaries. Sunday School teachers, home teachers, visiting teachers, Aaronic priesthood and Mutual leaders held exciting classes and implemented powerful member activation programs. At the end of the year, when the final reports were submitted, excitement and anticipation flamed through the stake. When the next list of outstanding stakes was published, heading the list was this rural stake in the mountains of Utah. The vision was fulfilled.

Outstanding leaders have lofty expectations and visions of great achievements. They envision clearly and precisely what the organization or activity should be like. Effective leaders must also understand the potential of their followers to contribute to achieving the envisioned goals. They know that the vision must include the followers.

As president of The Church of Jesus Christ of Latter-day Saints, Ezra Taft Benson saw the world flooded with copies of the Book of Mormon. That vision has stirred the imagination of millions of faithful followers. President Benson knew of their potential to accomplish the magnificent mission of every family in the Church contributing copies of the Book of Mormon to be distributed all over the world by missionaries and local Church leaders. Many families are collecting cards sent by missionaries about the reception of the Book of Mormon by nonmembers. The enactment of the vision is clearly contributing to the world at large and benefiting the growth and development of participating families.

Similarly, a Mormon temple presidency reported to President Spencer W. Kimball that they were number one in the Church in terms of activities taking place within the temple walls. Although President Kimball expressed deep appreciation, he knew the potential of the patrons to do even more, so he encouraged the temple presidency to "lengthen their stride."

A little branch of the Church in a southern community had an experienced leader who tried to implement the applicable Church policies and procedures. Needless to say, the vision was great, but implementation became a near disaster because of inexperienced followers—clearly a case of the leader getting too involved in the procedures without a realistic vision of the followers' strengths and weaknesses. But by keeping the vision bright and adjusting to the ability of members, the leader found his dream of achieving an excellent branch quickly moving forward. In a few years the branch became a fully staffed ward, meeting in a small beautiful chapel.

Leaders recognize that they and their associates have both strengths and weaknesses. Everyone has various gifts and talents. All have godlike potential. Leaders shape a vision of the future that capitalizes on what everyone brings to the situation. They also keep in mind what is best for the people in the organization.

Christ's example of leadership is positive, encouraging, and challenging. His vision included the idea that each follower has a yearning to succeed and, if it is required, they will accomplish the extraordinary. As leaders we too should have the same expectations of our followers. Leaders with a visionary purpose light the way so that others may see and follow. As with Christ, we too should say, "Come, follow me."

Constant Direction

Followers need a vision that will stir their imaginations and excite their souls. They also need to understand how to achieve the vision. They need to have specific, achievable, and practical goals to motivate them toward the larger vision and greater mission. Christ introduced a grand objective to his followers: "Be ye therefore perfect, even as your Father which is in heaven is perfect" (Matthew 5:48). That was the dream. Do not just be a good person, or only think about becoming a great teacher. Imagine becoming as perfect as Father in Heaven. Jesus urged, prodded, and invited his followers to steer consistently and persistently in a straight, narrow course that leads in one direction: toward perfection.

The Lord admonishes us to avoid distractions and avoid getting lost along the way by keeping in the center of the path. But how will we know when we are headed in the right direction or making any progress toward perfection? Jesus' explanation of how we should treat other people answers that question:

"Whosoever shall smite thee on thy right cheek, turn to him the other also. And if any man will sue thee at the law, and take away thy coat, let him have thy cloke also. And whosoever shall compel thee to go a mile, go with him twain. Give to him that asketh thee, and from him that would borrow of thee turn not thou away. Ye have heard that it hath been said, Thou shalt love thy neighbour, and hate thine enemy. But I say unto you, Love your enemies, bless them that curse you, do good to them that hate you, and pray for them which despitefully use you, and persecute you" (Matthew 5:39–44).

The vision is perfection; the goal is to love your enemies. Jesus told us how to accomplish the goal: turn your other cheek when the first is struck, walk two miles when compelled to walk one, and so forth.

A great leader needs a bright vision of what the organization and its members ought to be like and a clear idea of what is to be accomplished to achieve the vision. We call that a description of our desired direction. Sometimes it is called a mission statement.

The mission of Bonneville International Corporation, the Church's communications company, is to provide personal growth opportunities for employees, to enhance the effectiveness, power, influence, and value of properties, and to exert positive leadership in the broadcast industry (*BYU Today*, Nov. 1989, p. 34). The mission statement represents the vision translated into a direction and indicates what the organization is committed to do to bring about the vision.

A mission statement encapsulates and epitomizes the unique reason for the existence of the organization. The priesthood quorums of the Church, for example, derive their missions from two values: every individual is of immense worth, and each family in the Church is a government within itself (*Melchizedek Priesthood Personal Study Guide 1989*, p. 1). A priesthood quorum creates its mission, or purpose, from those two values. The mission unifies the organization and provides it with both a sense of direction and a rationale for its existence. The mission of a priesthood

40

quorum, using those two basic values, would be to strengthen every individual member of the quorum in order to enhance family leadership.

As leaders, we must set a course that is constant and clear in the minds of those with whom we work. The direction should not be vague or imprecise. The direction should be toward perfection. Once the vision is established, the direction we must go and the things we need to do must be understood if the vision is to be turned into a reality. After we envision the ideal Relief Society, priesthood quorum, family, or work team, we need to ask ourselves, "What do we need to accomplish to achieve the grand objective?"

A father and mother, concerned with influences outside of the home, wanted to have a unified family. They could easily imagine members of the family loving, supporting, and sustaining each other. The vision was clear. But how to achieve their goal would require more than hope that the family would become close and strong. This father and mother found it rather easy to love each other and be as one, because they were accustomed to talking frequently with each other. Whenever a problem arose, they took the time to counsel together and find a solution. Consequently, these parents decided that the whole family might benefit from talking frequently to each other and counseling together when concerns arise.

After some deliberation, the family agreed to hold a council and decide on a way to develop a closer family. It didn't take long for the younger members of the family to see the benefits of meeting together. They were able to help make important decisions, share their goals and dreams for the future, and seek the support and help of other family members to make their own difficulties and burdens a little lighter.

The first goal they agreed upon was to hold regular family home evenings. The second goal was to offer helpful suggestions and service to members of the family who were having a little difficulty in school. The third goal was to pray individually each day to Heavenly Father for direction and strength.

Other achievable goals were identified and plans were set. The vision of a happy, unified family was vividly described so that the children could not only share in the weekly goals and achievements but they could also feel part of something bigger and greater than themselves: an eternal, celestial family whose unity and love continues forever and ever.

Do not be discouraged if all of your goals are not immediately achieved. Accomplishing some of the goals is exciting and a sign that you have made a good start. We all like to feel that we are making progress. Little successes breed confidence and enthusiasm. To be associated with a successful organization is an exciting feeling. No business, educational institution, or family is yet perfect. Each can have a great vision of achievable goals and directions that give the members confidence in the future.

Speak with Conviction

The Savior used every opportunity to speak enthusiastically and passionately about his goals and aspirations. Matthew recounts how Jesus commanded the apostles to conduct their business: "Go not into the way of the Gentiles, and into any city of the Samaritans enter ye not: but go rather to the lost sheep of the house of Israel" (Matthew 10:5–6). You can feel his intensity as he directed them to "preach, saying, The kingdom of heaven is at hand." Listen carefully as Jesus urges them to be selective: "And whosoever shall not receive you, nor hear your words, when ye depart out of that house or city, shake off the dust of your feet" (Matthew 10:7, 14). These words were not spoken casually but uttered with conviction.

Corporate business leaders and great political leaders seize every opportunity to articulate their views over and over again to individuals and groups who will listen. Many leaders forget that it is as necessary to communicate the vision as it is to create the vision. A good idea doesn't run around by itself and find lodging in the hearts of people. A dream and its accompanying goals must be told and retold in every possible way. An American corporate president successfully used his personality and the various media to convey the mission of his company to employees and to the public at large. His dreams and hopes captured the imaginations of thousands of people. Subsequently, he was able to move his large company from a deficit financial position to a successful one.

How did the multitudes react to Christ as they listened to the Sermon on the Mount? We read in Matthew, "And it came to pass, when Jesus had ended these sayings, the people were astonished at his doctrine: for he taught them as one having authority, and not as the scribes" (Matthew 7:28–29). In like manner, President Harold B. Lee inspired members of the Church throughout the world when he exhorted everyone to "get and read the discourses that have been delivered at this conference; for what these brethren have spoken by the power of the Holy Ghost is the mind of the Lord, the will of the Lord, the voice of the Lord, and the power of God unto salvation" (in Conference Report, Apr. 1973, p. 176).

Since that time, greater efforts have been made to read and study General conference addresses in priesthood quo-

rum meetings, family gatherings, and Relief Society meetings. Home teachers have articulated the messages and the
spirit of conference to their families. Seminary and institute
of religion classes have studied and discussed the conference
addresses.

We can only conclude that leadership involves speaking
and communicating with conviction. The Spirit prompts us
to take our ideas and commitments out of our own minds
and hearts and then speak up to share those views with
others.

Jesus exhorted us in these words: "Ye are the light of
the world. A city that is set on an hill cannot be hid. Neither
do men light a candle, and put it under a bushel, but on a
candlestick; and it giveth light unto all that are in the house.
Let your light so shine before men, that they may see your
good works, and glorify your Father which is in heaven"
(Matthew 5:14–16).

Jesus explained that when we speak with the Spirit, we
will have the confidence to face difficult situations and to
speak with authority and conviction (see Matthew 10:19–
28). We can obtain confirmation from the Spirit concerning
what to say and how to say it. Elder Russell M. Nelson of
the Quorum of the Twelve Apostles describes what it is like
when we draw upon the Spirit:

"Friday evening before the Solemn Assembly, to be attended by all the priesthood leaders of fourteen stakes the
following morning, I was on an airplane with Sister Nelson
and with President Hinckley. I leaned over to him seated
right in front of me and I said, 'President, I'd be pleased to
receive whatever instructions you'd care to give me about
the subject matter, length of time. Whatever direction you
would like to give me—I'd be most grateful for it.' 'Please!'
he said, 'talk as long as you want on any subject you want.

You're the servant of the Lord. You give the message the Lord wants you to give.'

"We got to St. George to the motel about ten o'clock at night. I kissed my sweetheart goodnight, tucked her in, and then prayed. I don't think I went to bed that night. I sat up in that room poring over the scriptures, studying, searching, and writing. It came, and the following morning President Hinckley called on me to be the first speaker. I gave the message that came between midnight and 5:00 A.M." (*Melchizedek Priesthood Personal Study Guide 1989*, pp. 196–97).

Like Jesus, we too may have occasion to speak with conviction and to receive the same kind of reaction that the Savior did: "All the people were very attentive to hear him" (Luke 19:48).

The conviction and dynamism with which Christ spoke came from a deep-seated understanding of his divine calling. As mortals with knowledge of our divine inheritance, we too can speak with calm and dynamic insight. As leaders we have both the charge and the opportunity to follow the example of the Savior and speak out for good.

Not only must Christlike leaders speak with conviction, but they must also be prepared to respond to questions raised by followers. Christ, through confidence and calmness, conviction and understanding, could change a difficult situation into a moment of direction and focus. When performing miracles, Jesus was regularly challenged to justify his acts. Matthew recounts the healing of a man with a withered hand. The Pharisees were watching to see whether Jesus would heal the man. Their purpose was to accuse him of violating the sabbath. In a thinly veiled dialogue, the Pharisees challenged him with the question, "Is it lawful to heal on the sabbath days?" (Matthew 12:10).

His reply was neither condescending nor argumentative, but direct and gentle: "Is it lawful," he asked, "to do good on the sabbath days?" Then he broadened the issue by asking if it was lawful to do evil, to save life, or to kill (Mark 3:4).

Facing a restless group of learned antagonists, Jesus drove his point home with a provocative question-parable: "What man shall there be among you, that shall have one sheep, and if it fall into a pit on the sabbath day, will he not lay hold on it, and lift it out?" Then, the powerful conclusion is offered in simplicity but with conviction: "How much then is a man better than a sheep?" (Mark 3:11–12).

What did Jesus do then? Did he play to the crowd? Did he seek to retaliate because of their accusations? Did he chortle with his disciples? No. He quietly called upon the injured man and asked him to stretch forth his hand. Then he restored him to health. The issue was settled.

Another incident showing how Jesus was prepared to answer questions occured when on the sabbath he healed a woman who had been infirm for eighteen years. The ruler of the synagogue responded indignantly to the healing. Jesus answered with a firm and direct response: "Thou hypocrite, doth not each one of you on the sabbath loose his ox or his ass from the stall, and lead him away to watering? And ought not this woman . . . be loosed from this bond on the sabbath day?" (Luke 13:15–16).

Rather than argue with the ruler, Christ skillfully drew out a relevant answer with a carefully placed question. The challenge offered by the ruler was firmly diverted and captured as a strong reason for the Savior's actions.

To be effective leaders, parents must listen to the questions of children and respond to them with appropriate answers. Failing to give a response, or responding ambiguously, causes confusion and misunderstanding. In a family home evening, the children unanimously agreed that they would like to take a vacation to New England. They had been impressed at school with the events that had transpired in the founding of America in New England. When they queried their parents about the possibility of such a trip, they met an awkward silence and some incoherent comments about the costs of such a vacation.

The alert, optimistic smiles of the children quickly vanished, replaced by expressions of hurt and bewilderment. Later, they asked questions about whether Dad was seriously ill or Mom was expecting a baby. Why else would they not be encouraged to pursue such a magnificent vacation?

Perhaps the parents needed to share their real reasons for hesitating about such a marvelous and exciting trip. If costs were the problem, that might be remedied in a variety of ways, including taking a shorter trip with the same purpose.

In any case, parents, managers, church leaders, and anyone wanting to lead and influence people must respond to questions in the clearest, kindest, and most optimistic way possible. The Savior's perfect approach to leadership demonstrates that people will follow one who has an expressed, visionary purpose, who provides constant direction toward that purpose, and speaks with conviction.

Patient Instruction

As surely as we mortals tire, Jesus must have become weary of constantly explaining that he was the Christ, that he would die and be resurrected. His responses show that he was slightly provoked on occasion, as when he asked his disciples, "And why call ye me, Lord, Lord, and do not the things which I say?" (Luke 6:46). We see, however, the immediate unfolding of a lesson—in this case the story of the builder who built his house on a rock foundation in contrast to the person who built a house directly on the earth. The storm beat against it and it fell in ruin (Luke 6:48–49).

Christ's great leadership and attractiveness as one to be followed was demonstrated by his unerring patience in giving instructions. The scriptures show, directly and indirectly, that Jesus "went throughout every city and village, preaching and shewing the glad tidings of the kingdom of God: and the twelve were with him" (Luke 8:1). How was he received? Luke reports that "the people gladly received him: for they were all waiting for him" (Luke 8:40).

How did he approach the task of patient instruction? As Luke states, "he taught daily in the temple" (Luke 19:47). While teaching, he was sometimes harangued and challenged. When asked by feigning deceivers, "Is it lawful for us to give tribute unto Caesar, or no?" Jesus answered: "Render therefore unto Caesar the things which be Caesar's, and unto God the things which be God's." What type of reaction did his teaching bring? "And they could not take hold of his words before the people: and they marvelled at his answer, and held their peace" (Luke 20:25–26).

Patiently instructing all attentive listeners, counseling with his disciples, and directing his apostles, Jesus drew people to him. "And in the day time he was teaching in the temple; and at night he went out, and abode in the mount that is called the Mount of Olives. And all the people came early in the morning to him in the temple, for to hear him" (Luke 21:37–38). "And early in the morning, he came *again* into the temple, and all the people came unto him;

48

and he sat down, and taught them" (John 8:2; emphasis added).

Excellent examples of patient instruction are personified in the general authorities of the Church. They sometimes spend several days attending stake and regional conferences while instructing individuals, groups, and large audiences. Their aim is to illuminate the grand mission of the gospel and the Church and give directions for achieving goals along the way.

Elder Boyd K. Packer's excellent use of patient instruction makes him particularly receptive to questions from the Saints in conferences throughout the world. In a recent stake priesthood leadership meeting, Elder Packer asked the stake president to call the meeting to order, have the opening song and prayer, and then turn the time over to him. Elder Packer spoke briefly and then said that he would be happy to respond to any questions the brethren might have.

For about an hour and a half, Elder Packer listened attentively and thoroughly and clearly answered each question to the satisfaction of the questioner. "What is the biggest weakness of the Saints along the Wasatch Front?" "What should I do as elders quorum president when some of the faithful members do not attend the temple regularly?" "What is the responsibility of the bishop when some members of the ward do not respond to the pleading of the prophet to prepare their families for the perilous times that are rapidly approaching?"

When the meeting finally ended, stake priesthood leaders congregated in the hallways and commented about the marvelous individual instruction that each one had received from a general authority of the Church.

Jesus was untiring in his efforts to create the vision that would attract his followers. He was constant, never veering from the goal he pursued. He spoke enthusiastically, with power and conviction. Multitudes of people came to hear his message. And then with remarkable patience he instructed and guided his followers to a clear understanding of how to live life more abundantly. To be effective as leaders, we need to follow the Savior's example and learn how to create and communicate a lively vision for those whom we lead.

4

THE FOURTH KEY:
EMPOWER FOLLOWERS TO ACT

Jesus demonstrated the following simple and effective system for involving others in the work of the kingdom when he prepared the Twelve Apostles to begin their ministry.

Seven Steps

He called them together.

"Then he called his twelve disciples together" (Luke 9:1). Jesus used meetings to prepare others and involve them in the work. Calling people together, face to face, is essential to involve followers in the work.

He gave them power and authority.

"And [he] gave them power and authority" (Luke 9:1). Very few people feel comfortable in performing assignments until they have the authority to do so. Jesus prepared those he called to lead and set them apart to do the work.

He sent them.

"And he sent them to preach the kingdom of God, and to heal the sick" (Luke 9:2). Often we forget that even when

51

prepared individuals have the authority, they must be specifically instructed about how to get started.

He had them report to him.

"And the apostles, when they were returned, told him all that they had done" (Luke 9:10). When leaders delegate authority, power, and responsibilities, they must have a mechanism for learning how the assignments are carried out. The most efficient way is to ask for a report.

He took them aside privately.

"And he took them, and went aside privately" (Luke 9:10). Leadership involves leaders counseling privately with key members. Whether it is a work group, a quorum, or a family, problems can be reviewed and plans laid.

He counseled and planned with his immediate assistants.

"He took Peter and John and James, and went up into a mountain to pray" (Luke 9:28). Presidency meetings, committee meetings, planning sessions, family councils, and leadership meetings – all require meeting together in a private place.

After Jesus cast out the evil spirit from the young boy, "his disciples asked him privately, Why could not we cast him out?" (Mark 9:28). Jesus taught the disciples, counseled with them, and explained marvelous things. On one occasion he advised them that "blessed are your eyes, for they see: and your ears, for they hear. For verily I say unto you, That many prophets and righteous men have desired to see those things which ye see, and have not seen them; and to hear those things which ye hear, and have not heard them" (Matthew 13:16–17). Such was the way of the Perfect Leader to counsel and advise as well as to inform his disciples of privileged and sacred information.

Jesus trusted his followers and communicated with them frequently. The scriptures record often that Jesus called his disciples to him and taught them (see, for example, Matthew 15:32).

He sought new talent and additional followers.

"Therefore said he unto them, The harvest truly is great, but the laborers are few: pray ye therefore the Lord of the harvest, that he would send forth labourers into his harvest" (Luke 10:2). One important task of a leader is to recruit new members. A leader should select strong associates to guide the work. Jesus prayerfully searched for those who would become a faithful part of building the kingdom and strengthening the Saints.

Involving others in the work is an obvious leadership imperative. Followers who are involved in the work create enormous amounts of energy that propel everyone toward the vision. Jesus included his followers in the process of spreading the gospel. The Savior selected those who would help him, gave them important and specific things to do, instructed and advised them on how to carry out their assignments, and taught them the importance of accountability.

Organizations are formed, primarily, because one person acting alone can never accomplish complex goals that involve large numbers of tasks. In a university management class, a professor reminds students that by themselves they will accomplish far less than if they work with others, especially those who want to help develop and implement a product or a service. He further explains that everyone has a million-dollar idea, but statistically, no one in the class will ever become a millionaire. The reason is that most people will not implement their ideas. They just do not have the encouragement or resources to get their ideas to market.

Then the professor tells about his millionaire friend, who is very successful at implementing other people's ideas. The friend says, "Most people smile when they have a good idea, but I smile all the way to the bank." The professor concludes that in most circumstances, it is much wiser to share ideas, the work associated with implementing a good idea, and the rewards that result. It is better to have 10 percent of something than 100 percent of nothing.

A Simple Procedure

The quickest and most complete way to involve people and empower them to act is to give them something meaningful to do. A leader who wants to assign work in a way that motivates individuals to follow through properly should use this simple procedure:

Identify a specific individual.

Determine the person to whom you would like to delegate the assignment.

Give the whole picture.

Explain the setting and the circumstances under which the delegated assignment will take place. For example, you could say, "We will be taking fifteen minutes to commemorate the restoration of the Aaronic Priesthood at the beginning of our priesthood meeting Sunday. There will be three five-minute talks, and then we will separate into quorums."

Describe the need.

You might explain that "the first speaker will be the bishop, after which the teacher's quorum president will speak. What we really need in order to complete the program is a father who will share something that his family does together that builds family unity."

Share the decision.

Ask the individual, "As a father yourself, what have you done recently that seems to be something your family enjoys?" After he responds, ask, "Do you think you could share that idea with us this Sunday for four or five minutes?"

Emphasize the importance.

Be sure to stress the importance of what you are asking. "The fathers and sons are interested in what your family is doing because they admire how happily your family lives together. And you will be representing all the fathers of the ward."

Establish a trigger point.

Set a time, usually a day or two before the assignment is to be completed, when the individual can be called, reminded, and encouraged about the assignment. Set a time that is convenient to the individual. If you are a busy leader, you could assign an assistant to make the call. Inquire, "How is that talk coming for tomorrow in priesthood meeting? Is there anything further that you need to know about the meeting tomorrow?"

Follow up.

Either you or an assistant should make special note of how the assignment was handled. Be sure to give the individual an opportunity to report to you on the successful completion of the assignment.

Give recognition.

No matter how many times a person does an assignment, take the time to make each experience rewarding. If for no other reason than that you have been freed to do something else, you should give special recognition to the person doing the assignment. In the example we've been using, the father who gave the talk was presented a picture of the restoration of the Aaronic Priesthood inscribed with an expression of appreciation from the bishop.

Giving assignments to others demonstrates the trust and confidence leaders have in their followers. Delegation of tasks also gives individuals an opportunity to develop important capabilities and to increase knowledge. Delegation usually improves subordinates' morale and increases commitment because it allows them to help decide how to complete the work.

Effective leaders do not delegate just tasks. Sometimes it is more encouraging and exciting for an individual to research an idea and write a report. If a follower looks a little bored, we can ask the person to explore a new work approach and to prepare some advice on the matter. The point is that as leaders, we need to keep people moving and contributing. Once followers feel a lack of forward motion, they quickly become bored and less productive. Leaders cannot afford to wait around until followers energize themselves. They must use every means possible to keep followers involved and on fire.

Although Jesus was able to perform miracles directly, he often involved the person to be healed. Miracles are often preceded by indications of faith. According to Elder James E. Talmage, Jesus refused to commit himself to those whose belief was based solely on miracles: "Our Lord would not regard miracles, though wrought by Himself, as a sufficient and secure foundation of faith" (*Jesus the Christ*, p. 177).

Invite People to Be Involved

It was essential that the disciple be involved in the miracle, at least to the extent of demonstrating a trusting faith. Peter, for example, was invited to walk on the sea. To accomplish that feat, the scriptures record, Jesus said, "Come," and when Peter came down from the ship, he walked on the water (Matthew 14:22–33).

At the feeding of the five thousand, Jesus blessed the food and then "gave the loaves to his disciples, and the disciples to the multitude" (Matthew 14:19). An orderly process of delegation was involved, with the disciples being directly involved in the miracle. In addition, as Mark explains, the large number of people were organized and given assignments: Jesus "commanded them to make all sit down by companies upon the green grass. And they sat down in ranks, by hundreds, and by fifties" (Mark 6:39–40).

Great leaders devise ways to organize work and involve their followers in accomplishing assignments. The Savior constantly involved others by giving specific assignments.

The second feeding of a large multitude of people was handled in about the same way as the feeding of the five thousand. Jesus called his disciples around him and explained that he did not want the crowd to be sent away without eating. He asked the disciples how many loaves of bread and how much other food they had. Then he directed the multitude to sit on the ground. He blessed the food and "gave to his disciples, and the disciples to the multitude" (Matthew 15:36).

Jesus taught the disciples by involving them personally in the work. The Savior's actions about a tribute payment in Capernaum show us ways to engage people by giving them specific assignments: "And when they were come to Capernaum, they that received tribute money came to Peter, and said, Doth not your master pay tribute? He saith, Yes. And when he was come into the house, Jesus prevented him, saying, . . . Notwithstanding, lest we should offend them, go thou to the sea, and cast an hook, and take up the fish that first cometh up; and when thou hast opened his mouth, thou shalt find a piece of money: that take, and give unto them for me and thee" (Matthew 17:24–27).

Jesus could have provided the coin without the intense involvement of Peter's getting his fishing gear, catching a fish, finding the coin, and taking it to the tax collector. But Peter learned from the experience, and his faith was strengthened.

An older home teacher asked his young companion to offer a prayer before they began their visiting. As soon as the younger companion was comfortable with praying, the senior companion asked him to give a short part of the message to each family they visited. Soon the younger companion became confident in that task, and then he learned how to pray with the families and to give the whole lesson. His next step was to schedule appointments and ask the head of each household what message or assistance would be most appropriate for the family.

"Success breeds success." "Inch by inch, life's a cinch." These sayings express exactly what happened when the sen-

58

ior home teacher helped his younger companion to succeed. In no time this young Aaronic Priesthood holder was bragging a little to his quorum buddies that "home teaching is a piece of cake, if you know what you are doing."

Stimulate and Provoke Others

Involvement consists of much more than encouraging and inviting others to participate in activities. Involvement has an emotional side to it, too. To be involved is to "feel" the challenge and the excitement of an event. When their emotions are stimulated, participants are carried forward into action. Jesus suggested that point indirectly when he asked the disciples: "Suppose ye that I am come to give peace on earth? I tell you, Nay: but rather division" (Luke 12:51).

Jesus actively involved others. He challenged traditions and, as illustrated in the hearing before Pilate, he was criticized that "he stirreth up the people." Jesus was constantly stimulating and provoking people to keep moving.

Jesus asked for strong commitments, of course, and we should do the same. "So likewise, whosoever he be of you that forsaketh not all that he hath, he cannot be my disciple" (Luke 14:33). Certainly that injunction suggests that leaders should have plans, goals, and expectations.

Lack of commitment is demonstrated by broken appointments or incomplete assignments. The Savior taught, "No man, having put his hand to the plough, and looking back, is fit for the kingdom of God" (Luke 9:62). From time to time, some of Christ's would-be followers came and went. John reports that "many of his disciples went back, and walked no more with him." Even the apostles were questioned about their loyalty: "Then said Jesus unto the twelve, Will ye also go away?" The impetuous Peter immediately declared, "Lord, to whom shall we go? thou hast the words of eternal life" (John 6:66–68).

Stay Close

Involving and encouraging people requires that we work closely with them. Jesus and his disciples walked together, worked together, ate together, shared experiences together, and encouraged one another. Throughout the scriptures we read such phrases as these:

"And both Jesus was called, and his disciples, to the marriage" (John 2:2).

"After this he went down to Capernaum, he, and his mother, and his brethren, and his disciples" (John 2:12).

"After these things came Jesus and his disciples into the land of Judea" (John 3:22).

"And Jesus went up into a mountain, and there he sat with his disciples" (John 6:3).

"Jesus therefore walked no more openly among the Jews; but went thence unto a country near to the wilderness, into a city called Ephraim, and there continued with his disciples" (John 11:54).

Even though the customs of that time did not encourage socializing between men and women, Jesus was equally comfortable with both sexes in public and private. Both males and females sought instruction from him and could speak to him with ease. He was quite friendly with the innocent children. Although he was a Jew, he found good in the Samaritan and faith in the Roman centurion (Matthew 8:10). Social status and class rank did not matter. Christ stayed close to his followers, especially his designated Twelve Apostles.

The Savior frequently talked with the apostles apart from the rest of the multitude. He was no doubt advising, teaching, and admonishing. His task was to help them develop the knowledge, skills, and attitudes necessary to carry on the work. Christ had to prepare them for a tempest of opposition and rejection, as well as teach them how to succeed by drawing upon inner power. The disciples would be persecuted, face ostracism, be brought to trial, and be hated by many (Mark 13:9–13). They needed the ability and strength to continue forward when their leader was not with them. Christ was definitely not a long-distance leader or an absentee manager. He constantly directed and supported his followers.

As leaders, it is our task to help develop the people with whom we work. That development happens when we meet with them, teach them, advise them, and express adequate appreciation to them. During a discussion among a group of students studying important leadership skills that managers should know, management by objectives (MBO) was mentioned. A student mentioned management by walking around (MBWA). Soon everyone was using similar abbreviations — MBTAI for management by talking about it, and MBTP for management by thinking positively.

Near the conclusion of this creative sojourn into the realms of humanistic leadership, a student who had been reading about the life of Christ suggested that you would not be following Christ's example of leadership unless you LBET — lead by eating together. After a round of laughter, the would-be scholars agreed that Christ enhanced his leadership success by working, walking, eating, talking, and probably sharing some humor about the daily happenings in Jerusalem with his followers.

Sometimes the only way to direct a teenager is to talk together while working on a project or sharing insights while eating someplace. Leaders who share a meal and conversation with their followers are not surprised at the under-standing, trust, and loyalty that develop from such a simple activity.

The greatest lesson of close leadership is offered from the last days of Christ's life when he sat with the apostles during the Passover. Luke explains that "there was also a strife among them, which of them should be accounted the greatest" (Luke 22:24). In response to the bickering, Jesus explained his philosophy of leadership: "The kings of the Gentiles exercise lordship over them; and they that exercise authority upon them are called benefactors. But ye shall not be so: but he that is greatest among you, let him be as the younger; and he that is chief, as he that doth serve" (Luke 22:27).

Jesus counseled further, "When thou art converted, strengthen thy brethren" (Luke 22:32). We can learn to lead through service—by providing strength and power to those with whom we work.

And thus we see that great leaders do not dominate their followers. Rather, they set direction and tone while stim-ulating enthusiasm and involvement. The best leaders en-vision the future of a group or organization and attract others to participate. Perfect leadership, as portrayed by Christ, invites people to be involved, helps them feel the involve-ment, and stays close to them while they are involved. In that way, leaders transmit the power and the authority to their followers to carry out the work.

5

THE FIFTH KEY:
STRENGTHEN YOURSELF, PART 1

Late one afternoon after a work-filled day, Jesus and his disciples boarded a small ship to cross the Sea of Galilee. As the boat set sail, Jesus fell asleep near the ship's stern. "And behold, there arose a great tempest in the sea, insomuch that the ship was covered with the waves: but he was asleep" (Matthew 8:24).

That circumstance, according to Elder James E. Talmage, helps us understand the reality of Christ's physical attributes and the healthy condition of his body: "He was subject to fatigue and bodily exhaustion from other causes, as are all men; without food He grew hungry; without drink He thirsted; by labor He became weary. The fact that after a day of strenuous effort He could calmly sleep, even amidst the turmoil of a tempest, indicates an unimpaired nervous system and a good state of health. Nowhere do we find record of Jesus having been ill. He lived according to the laws of health, yet never allowed the body to rule the spirit; and His daily activities, which were of a kind to make heavy demands on both physical and mental energy, were met with no symptoms of nervous collapse nor of functional disturbance.

Sleep after toil is natural and necessary. The day's work done, Jesus slept" (*Jesus the Christ*, pp. 307–8).

To lead others tirelessly, patiently, and effectively, through periods of disappointment and fatigue, requires that we master the basic principles of personal regeneration and self-renewal. Absolutely nothing in scriptural records allows us to imagine Jesus as a sad, gloomy, fatigued, depressed, and overburdened person. It is equally impossible to picture Jesus with his robes flying as he rushes thither and yon, helter-skelter, trying to accomplish twenty things at once. Although we see many who look disheveled as they rush through their daily agendas, such was not the strong, calm, and steady example set by the Man from Galilee.

Though Jesus' life was dedicated to serving and leading people, he did not ignore opportunities to relax with friends, eat nourishing food, or sleep after a day of work. Observance of the laws of health, together with the proper use of faith and prayer, does much to lift our spirits. Finding joy in attending to others' needs, resisting the appearance of busyness, and concentrating on one thing at a time help to renew our inner strength.

The Lord's Law of Health

Throughout history, the Lord has instructed his people concerning their health. Adam was introduced to the best use of crops and herbs (Genesis 1:29–36). Noah and Moses were taught about various herbs and meats (Genesis 9:3–4); Deuteronomy 14:2–3). Daniel and his companions received special direction about what to eat in the house of the king of Babylon (Daniel 1). In modern times, a revelation in the Doctrine and Covenants is frequently referred to as the Lord's law of health and is called the Word of Wisdom (D&C 89). The Lord has given principles of health and well-being in other sections of the Doctrine and Covenants, the Book of Mormon, and the New Testament (see, for example, D&C 10:4; 49:19; 59:16–20; 88:124; Alma 46:40; Ephesians 5:18; Acts 27:34).

The scriptures do not detail everything we should and should not eat or drink. The Lord has warned us about certain foods and substances that are not good for us. He has given us a way to better resist disease by living these revelations. His guidelines help us choose wisely what to eat, drink, or take into our bodies in every situation.

Isn't it interesting that scholars and researchers worldwide are now teaching many of the same ideas about sleep that the Lord revealed to Joseph Smith? "Cease to sleep longer than is needful," says the Lord. "Retire to thy bed early, that ye may not be weary; arise early, that your bodies and your minds may be invigorated" (D&C 88:124).

The mind and the body are connected. Textbooks that recognize this relationship between mind and body are often called "physiological psychology," or "psychological physiology." They demonstrate the effect of the body on the mind, and vice versa. The Lord already knows all about the effects – after all, he created us. He does not tell us at what hour to retire and at what hour to arise, nor does he tell us the total number of hours we should sleep each night in order to feel invigorated. Nevertheless, he has given us correct principles and guidelines, and we are expected to use them wisely. We need to base our judgments on these revealed truths and make our own decisions.

Some years ago in a general conference address, President Ezra Taft Benson suggested that for our well-being, "rest and physical exercise are essential, and a walk in the fresh air can refresh the spirit. Wholesome recreation is part of our religion, and a change of pace is necessary, and even its anticipation can lift the spirit" (in Conference Report, Oct. 1974, p. 92).

The mental and spiritual aspects of yielding obedience to God's laws of health in following the Word of Wisdom are summarized rather succinctly by Elder Stephen L Richards, then a member of the Quorum of the Twelve Apostles: "The largest measure of good derived from its observance is in increased faith and the development of more spiritual power and wisdom" (in Conference Report, Apr. 1949, p. 141).

The Power of Faith

Faith helps us to overcome difficulties. It controls doubts and fears that we sometimes experience when we are trying to lead effectively. The Savior assured us of the powerful possibilities of faith when he said, "Verily I say unto you, If ye have faith as a grain of mustard seed, ye shall say unto this mountain, Remove hence to yonder place; and it shall remove; and nothing shall be impossible unto you" (Matthew 17:20). The literal meaning of that statement is stunning. To think that just a tiny bit of faith could move something as large as a mountain staggers the mind. But to us as leaders, even the figurative meaning of moving a mountain, which means overcoming a major difficulty, is equally awesome to imagine.

The Gospels are replete with stories of Jesus' ability to remain calm and in control while dealing with difficult situations; however, few insights are more instructive than Jesus' stilling the tempest. During the evening, Jesus and his disciples were sailing across the Sea of Galilee. A furious storm came up quickly, tossing their small ship mercilessly upon the waves until the water came over the sides. Jesus slept peacefully, and though the apostles were well ac-

66

quainted with the sudden storms and the wind-lashed waves of this body of water, they became frightened. At last, each moment threatening their utter destruction, they awakened Jesus with the cry: "Lord, save us: we perish." Without alarm and with amazing self-control, Jesus quietly appraised the situation. His only question was, "Why are ye fearful, O ye of little faith? Then he arose, and rebuked the winds and the sea; and there was a great calm" (Matthew 8:25–26).

On another occasion Jesus crossed the waters to escape the crowds, find seclusion, and seek a time to rest. The departure of Jesus and the Twelve was observed by an enthusiastic crowd of five thousand. They ran along the shore, around the end of the lake, and arrived at the landing place. Jesus and his companions were "moved with compassion toward them," taught them, and administered to their afflictions (Matthew 14:14). In the late hours of the day, Jesus performed the miracle of the loaves and fishes by feeding the multitude and even gathered twelve baskets of surplus.

Jubilant, the crowds proposed proclaiming Jesus their king. Knowing their intentions and realizing that his whole messianic mission could be thwarted in one short moment, Jesus sent his disciples away by boat while he stayed to disperse the excited crowd. When his disciples were safely journeying across the lake, Jesus cleared up the crowd's misconceptions. Then he ascended a hill and secluded himself in prayer during most of the night.

As fate would have it, the disciples' boat trip met with near disaster. "The ship was now in the midst of the sea, tossed with waves; for the wind was contrary" (Matthew 14:24). The crew labored hard most of the night to keep the ship from being wrecked but made very little progress on their journey.

Jesus, though secluded from his disciples, knew of their peril. "And in the fourth watch of the night Jesus went unto them, walking on the sea. And when the disciples saw him walking on the sea, they were troubled, saying, It is a spirit; and they cried out for fear. But straightway Jesus spake unto them, saying, Be of good cheer; it is I; be not afraid. And Peter answered him and said, Lord, if it be thou, bid me come unto thee on the water. And he said, Come. And when Peter was come down out of the ship, he walked on the water, to go to Jesus. But when he saw the wind boisterous, he was afraid; and beginning to sink, he cried, saying, Lord, save me. And immediately Jesus stretched forth his hand, and caught him, and said unto him, O thou of little faith, wherefore didst thou doubt? And when they were come into the ship, the wind ceased" (Matthew 14:25–32).

These marvelous demonstrations of faith show us that even natural forces can be controlled with great spiritual power. Of equal importance is Peter's remarkable experience. Always somewhat impetuous, Peter is to be commended for at least trying to duplicate the miraculous feat of his Master. When Peter requested the opportunity to walk on the waves, Jesus assented and said to him, "Come." The scriptures record that Peter walked on the water, but when he became afraid, he began to sink. Nevertheless, Peter proved that with sufficient faith in the Lord, walking on water could be done.

Two missionaries in Samoa were preparing for a meeting with investigators. Having felt the Spirit during previous visits with several families, they wanted to invite them to listen to the message of the gospel and ask questions about

The Church of Jesus Christ of Latter-day Saints. At that time, the ministers from the predominant churches in the village had sent word that no members of any congregation were to let the Mormon missionaries into their homes. They were also forbidden to attend any meeting the missionaries held.

The missionaries felt that it was their duty to let all the villagers know that the gospel had been restored and that baptism could be administered only by servants of the Lord who held the proper authority. So they decided to walk up to the entrance of each Samoan house and give their message.

The Samoan homes were oval-shaped, with poles set in the ground four or five feet apart to support the dome-shaped, thatched roof. During the day, the walls, which were thatched-leaf blinds, were pulled up so as to expose most of the activities inside. Thus, even though the missionaries were sometimes not invited into a house, they were able to deliver their message to the parents and children inside. The missionaries aroused considerable curiosity about the meeting, and when the appointed hour arrived for the meeting to begin, the meetinghouse was filled to capacity.

The meeting place was about the size of several Samoan houses, but sheets of tin covered the layer of woven leaves that formed the roof. As the meeting began, rain started to fall. Samoa receives some of the heaviest rains in the world. When a rain comes, it is as if someone had turned on a million water faucets. The force of the rain hitting the roof was awesome, but the sound was worse. The large raindrops splattering on the tin roof were like hundreds of drumsticks playing a drum roll on top of a giant tin can. The sound was so loud that it stopped the meeting. No one could hear the message of the young Mormon elders.

Some superstitious investigators thought that the interruption was providential and a possible warning to disband the meeting and return home. The missionary who was conducting the meeting waited for a short time to see if the rain would stop. It did not. As the noisy rain continued, the audience grew more restless. The missionaries were visibly shaken, feeling that they had overcome great odds and spent much time arranging for the meeting only to have their plans ruined by Mother Nature.

For a few minutes, the two elders discussed the gravity of their situation. They had great faith in Jesus Christ and wanted to proclaim his message to this group of Samoans. They had recently been taught by President David O. McKay that "man's extremity is the Lord's opportunity." If we go as far as we can to render service or preach the gospel and are confronted by an obstacle, the Lord will open a way to complete the task.

With considerable fear and trembling, the senior elder quietly stepped outside. The rain was coming down in torrents, pounding and rattling the metal roof. Humbly and undauntedly, the missionary raised his arms and implored the Lord to stop the rain. In his own human way, he reminded the Lord that these people had gathered together to learn the gospel and the plan of salvation. He told the Lord that he did not know what to do and that the matter was now in the Lord's hands. Before the elder could step back inside, the rain stopped and the noise ceased.

Speaking of the necessity of faith, the Prophet Joseph Smith said: "Because faith is wanting, the fruits are. No man since the world was had faith without having something along with it. The ancients quenched the violence of fire, escaped the edge of the sword, women received their dead, etc. By faith the worlds were made. A man who has none of the gifts has no faith; and he deceives himself, if he supposes he has. Faith has been wanting, not only among the heathen, but in professed Christendom also, so that tongues, healings, prophecy, and prophets and apostles, and all the gifts and blessings have been wanting" (*Teachings of the Prophet Joseph Smith*, p. 270).

Not only can faith be used to control the forces of nature, but faith can also be used to calm and quiet our hearts. Through faith, fear can be traded for confidence and despair turned into hope. Indeed, through faith we can be renewed.

A missionary was explaining the restoration of the gospel to a group of skeptical Polynesians. The missionary enthusiastically proclaimed that the power and gifts of ancient times had been brought forth again in these latter-days. He proclaimed that he held the same priesthood and authority as Jesus Christ.

In the rear of the hall, young people began to whisper and giggle among themselves. Finally, one person spoke out. "If you have the power of God, then perform a little miracle instead of merely talking about it." Others of the crowd quickly chimed in, "Yes, do something so we can believe in what you are saying."

The missionary was taken aback. For a moment he seemed to lose his composure. He struggled with the idea that giving signs did not build strong testimonies. Yet he was being challenged to do something that would open the hearts of his listeners to the remainder of his message.

His heart was racing. Seconds seemed to turn into hours. Suddenly, everyone could see perspiration forming on his flushed face. The situation seemed similar to the confrontation described in the Book of Mormon when Korihor said to Alma:

"If thou wilt show me a sign, that I may be convinced

that there is a God, yea, show unto me that he hath power, and then will I be convinced of the truth of thy words.

"But Alma said unto him: Thou hast had signs enough; will ye tempt your God? Will ye say, Show unto me a sign, when ye have the testimony of all these thy brethren, and also all the holy prophets? The scriptures are laid before thee, yea, and all things denote there is a God; yea, even the earth, and all things that are upon the face of it, yea, and its motion, yea, and also all the planets which move in their regular form do witness that there is a Supreme Creator" (Alma 30:43–44).

Korihor declined to believe that there is a God and insisted on a sign. Alma then gave a sign, which was that Korihor should be struck dumb. Korihor was stunned that he could not speak, but he also had to endure being "cast out, and went about from house to house begging for his food" (Alma 30:56).

Filled with the inspiration of an idea, the faithful missionary, with considerable calm and control, humbly approached his unbelieving audience. He explained that he felt impressed to respond to their request for a sign. He looked directly at the most vocal of the group and said, "All of you who would like to lose your eyesight for the remainder of your lives, please stand."

The audience was paralyzed by his startling announcement. The missionary was serious. He did not move or shift his gaze away from them. For a moment, it seemed like the whole world stood still. There was absolute silence. No one moved. No one talked.

Several moments passed. The challenge of a sign had been met. No one stood up, and no one spoke. The silence was finally broken by the missionary, who continued to explain that the gospel had been restored with all the power, gifts, and blessings of ancient times.

How to Strengthen Our Faith

Unquestionably, faith is a principle of power, a gift that we all should cultivate. For leaders, faith provides another way to bless people's lives, remove obstacles, and strengthen them.

The Prophet Joseph Smith taught in *Lectures on Faith* that "when a man works by faith he works by mental exertion instead of physical force" (p. 61). The mind is the essential part of us that perceives, feels, thinks, and wills. Out of our testimony and knowledge of Jesus Christ and obedience to his dictates, we exercise faith by willingly and strongly desiring something good and right to happen.

President John Taylor said that faith comes by "hearing the word of God dispensed by a living oracle or minister of God, clothed upon with power from on high" (*Gospel Kingdom*, p. 332). All of us know that our faith and our testimonies grow stronger when we hold church callings, go to the temple, pay tithing, do home teaching and visiting teaching, and serve others.

The Savior told his apostles that to have faith sufficiently strong to cast out devils requires the addition of fasting and prayer (Mark 9:14–29).

Elder Talmage indicated that prayer, fasting, and faith are related. He explained that faith can be used to strengthen and benefit oneself: "The Savior's statement concerning the evil spirit that the apostles were unable to subdue — 'Howbeit this kind goeth not out but by prayer and fasting' — indicates gradation in the malignity and evil power of demons, and gradation also in the results of varying degrees of faith. The apostles who failed on the occasion referred to had been able to cast out demons at other times. Fasting, when practised in prudence, and genuine prayer are conducive to the development of faith with its accompanying power for good. Individual application of this principle may be made with profit. Have you some besetting weakness, some sinful indulgence that you have vainly tried to overcome? Like the malignant demon that Christ rebuked in the boy, your sin may be of a kind that goeth out only through prayer and fasting" (*Jesus the Christ*, p. 395, n. 2).

As leaders and parents, we can use faith to intercede on behalf of others. The centurion whose faith was commended by Jesus pleaded not for himself but for his servant (Matthew 8:5–13). Jairus implored Jesus to intervene on behalf of a dying daughter (Luke 8:41–56). A Canaanite woman needed help for an afflicted daughter (Matthew 15:22–28).

With strong faith in the Lord, we can directly help others by giving a blessing or removing an obstacle. We can also give support and encouragement as well as help indirectly by interceding with the Lord on behalf of others.

Late one night a faithful mother of three children was faced with a desperate situation. Her three-year-old daughter lay extremely ill. Earlier that day, a doctor visited the house and examined the sick child. Pneumonia was the diagnosis. He could only give instructions for making her comfortable but could do nothing to alleviate the illness. The doctor left with considerable concern showing in his face and in the solemnity of his voice. He promised that he would check back the next day.

The elders had also administered to the sick child. The father was not a member of the Church at the time, and the family lived in an area of New England where there were few Church members and even fewer priesthood holders.

Awakening in the night, the mother crossed to the child's bed and anxiously peered down at the child. She could not detect any breathing. Filled with fear, the mother dropped to her knees and pleaded with the Lord to spare the child's life.

This woman had been an instrument in converting others to the gospel. She had studied the scriptures almost every day of her life. She tried to be a good leader and a good influence on those who came within her sphere of influence. She was a faithful servant of the Lord using her great faith on behalf of her seemingly lifeless daughter.

Arising from her prayer, the mother picked up the still and limp little body of her child and started shaking it. Still pleading with the Lord, the mother continued to shake the child until, finally, the child opened her eyes and started breathing regularly.

The next day, the doctor returned. Fearing the worst, he quietly asked about the condition of the little child.

The mother said, "Why don't you step into the bedroom and see for yourself?" Upon entering the room, the doctor was astonished to see the bright-eyed little girl sitting up in bed, coloring a picture.

The doctor explained that he had never seen anyone with pneumonia move from deathly ill to recovery in such a short period of time. Shaking his head in disbelief, he asked, "What happened? What happened here last night?"

Every valiant leader feels frustration and fatigue. When almost overcome with a never-ending struggle, everyone seeks refuge from the storm. To those who toil with faith, the promise is given: "Ask, and it shall be given you; seek, and ye shall find; knock, and it shall be opened unto you" (Matthew 7:7).

That is a real promise packed with real power. If we "ask with a sincere heart, with real intent, having faith in Christ," we will be strengthened (Moroni 10:4). As with Peter and other faithful disciples in the midst of the worst imaginable circumstances, we too can be reassured by the comforting voice of the Lord Jesus Christ saying, "Be of good cheer; it is I; be not afraid" (Matthew 14:27).

6

THE FIFTH KEY:
STRENGTHEN YOURSELF, PART 2

Jesus always found time for meditation and prayer. His entire ministry was punctuated with moments spent away from the crowds and his chosen disciples. He prayed, pondered his mission, and received great spiritual strength.

Pray Constantly

Although Jesus knew the purpose of his work and the direction he should go, he nevertheless prayed constantly. For example, after feeding the five thousand and before rescuing his frightened disciples from a capsizing boat, Matthew records that when Jesus "had sent the multitudes away, he went up into a mountain apart to pray: and when the evening was come, he was there alone" (Matthew 14:23).

Jesus must have prayed for several hours. He probably prayed for his followers, who were soon to be asked, "Whom say ye that I am?" He wanted them to survive every challenge and crisis, for he knew that they would have to lead from the moment of his departure. During his hours of prayer Jesus became aware of the impending disaster facing his disciples. So, "in the fourth watch of the night, Jesus went unto them, walking on the sea" (Matthew 14:25). Christ was concerned enough about his followers to walk directly across the water to the boat.

Christ's impressions about the boat's impending crisis and his decision to help the disciples occurred during a period of intense prayer. Jesus was prayerfully inspired to walk immediately to the storm-tossed vessel.

Renewed Strength Comes through Prayer

Marion G. Romney, a counselor in the First Presidency of the Church, spoke of the Savior's life and example: "Finally, and most importantly, I learned that he communed constantly with his Father through prayer. This he did not only to learn the will of his Father, but also to obtain the strength to do his Father's will" ("What Would Jesus Do?" *New Era*, Sept. 1972, p. 5).

Praying to learn the will of Heavenly Father and then asking for the strength to press forward even when the day is long and the work is hard is one of the ways that Jesus was able to strengthen and renew himself. Luke records that between the commotion caused by Jesus' healing on the Sabbath a man whose right hand was withered and the task of choosing twelve apostles from among his disciples, Jesus went out into a mountain to pray, and continued all night in prayer to God. Renewed and refreshed when the daylight came, Jesus called all his disciples to him and chose twelve, whom he named apostles. Then he came down with them and met a great multitude of people from Judea and Jerusalem. He spent the entire day teaching them and healing those who had diseases (Luke 6:6–13).

What an incredible series of events compressed into such a short period of time. Yet Jesus had the strength to carry on important activities all day, all night, and all the following day.

In a quorum meeting a Melchizedek priesthood holder who had been asked to describe what he did to keep himself close to the Lord, explained: "The single, most effective thing that I do to stay close to the Lord, beyond trying to keep the commandments, is to pray twice before I go to work."

That first sentence, phrased rather simply, seemed to capture everyone's interest. He explained that he usually arose before anyone else in his family between 5:30 and 6:00 in the morning. He quietly slipped into the bathroom to shave, making sure his eyes were at least partially open so that he wouldn't cut himself. After he shaved, he flossed and brushed his teeth and then, before showering, he knelt in prayer. He said that he always whispered his prayer loud enough so that he could hear what he was saying.

"Take Friday morning, for example. The fulness of my heart was overflowing. I was so grateful to be alive and to have the comfort and guidance that the gospel brings. My prayer is usually over in about forty-five seconds to a minute, but this time it seemed like an hour. I expressed deep appreciation for the consciousness of life that is in me and the direction that the gospel provides for my life.

"I also explained to the Lord two or three things that I wanted to accomplish before the day ended, tasks beyond those that are expected of me, and prayed for the necessary strength to accomplish them. For example, I needed to fill all of my assignments connected with teaching at the university, but I reviewed with the Lord my desire to finish writing a chapter for a new book and to make arrangements for a management seminar for an out-of-state nursing association.

"When I finish praying the first time, I have a relaxing,

warm shower and review the activities of the day. Often when I am in this calm condition, I receive insights into what should be said or done to make each activity of the day go more smoothly.

"After a pleasant shower, I go into my closet to get dressed. Once again, I kneel down and whisper a prayer. This second prayer is to see if I can even remember what I asked about in the first place. I feel strongly that I have too often prayed and then forgotten what I prayed about. By praying twice, I become more committed to what I truly need help with for the day.

"I leave my closet with strength and encouragement that I know what I am going to accomplish. When evening comes, I will be able to feel and express great appreciation to the Lord for sustaining my efforts."

During the hours of the Savior's greatest agony, he found a place of seclusion in the Garden of Gethsemane. He had been there before. His disciples followed him, and Jesus "said unto them, Pray that ye enter not into temptation."

Then he left them, knelt down, "and prayed, saying, Father, if thou be willing, remove this cup from me; nevertheless, not my will, but thine be done." His divine mission would end with incomprehensible suffering and, Luke tells us, in response to his prayer, "there appeared an angel unto him from heaven, strengthening him" (Luke 22:40–43).

The New Testament contains numerous references to the ministering of angels. Angels attended Jesus throughout his life on earth. Angels, messengers of the Lord, are spoken of as "ministering spirits" (Hebrews 1:14). More information about the work of angels and the difference between angels of the Lord and the spirits that followed Satan can be found in the Doctrine and Covenants and the Book of Mormon.

President John Taylor taught that "the action of the angels, or messengers of God, upon our minds, so that the heart can conceive things past, present, and to come, and revelations from the eternal world, is, among a majority of mankind, a greater mystery than all the secrets of philosophy, literature, superstition, and bigotry put together. . . .

"But, without going into any particular detail of the offices and duties of the different grades of angels, let us close by saying that the angels gather the elect, and pluck out all that offends" (*Gospel Kingdom*, p. 31).

For our purposes, suffice it to say that prayer can strengthen us through the inspiration of the Spirit and ministering of Angels.

Clear Impressions Come When We Are Relaxed

The efficacy of Jesus' example of prayer and the spirit of communion manifest in his daily life is further detailed by a remarkable experience recounted by Elder Harold B. Lee to seminary and institute teachers gathered at Brigham Young University:

"A few weeks ago, President McKay related to the Twelve an interesting experience, and I asked him yesterday if I might repeat it to you this morning. He said, 'It is a great thing to be responsive to the whisperings of the Spirit, and we know that when these whisperings come, it is a gift and our privilege to have them. They come when we are relaxed and not under pressure of appointments.' I want you to mark that. The President then took occasion to relate an experience in the life of Bishop John Wells, former member of the Presiding Bishopric. Brother John Wells was a great detail man and prepared many of the reports we are following up now. His boy was run over by a freight train. Sister Wells was inconsolable. She mourned during the three days prior to the funeral, received no comfort at the funeral, and was in a rather serious state of mind. One day soon after the funeral services, while she was lying on her bed, relaxed, still mourning, she says that her son appeared to her and said, 'Mother, do not mourn, do not cry. I am all right.' He told her that she did not understand how the accident happened and explained that he had given the signal to the engineer to move on, and then made the usual effort to catch the railing on the freight train. It was clearly an accident. Now listen! He said that as soon as he realized that he was in another environment, he tried to see his father, *but he couldn't reach him. His father was so busy with the duties in his office, he could not respond to his call.* Therefore, he had come to his mother. He said to her, 'You tell father that all is well with me, and I want you not to mourn anymore.'

" . . . President [McKay] made the statement that the point he had in mind was that when we are relaxed, in a private room, we are more susceptible to those things, and that, so far as he was concerned, his best thoughts come after he gets up in the morning and is relaxed and thinking about the duties of the day; that impressions come more clearly, as if it were to hear a voice. Those impressions are right. If we are worried about something and upset in our feelings, the inspiration does not come. If we so live that our minds are free from worry and our conscience is clear and our feelings are right toward one another, the operation of the spirit of the Lord upon our spirit is as real as when we pick up the telephone; but when they come, we must be brave enough to take the suggested actions. The Lord will approve it and the brethren will approve it, and we know it is right.

"He said, 'It is a great consolation in this upset world today to know that our Savior is directing this work.' Then the President concluded: 'I value that testimony.' If you forget all else I have said, you remember that lesson and admonition" (address to LDS seminary and institute of religion teachers, 6 July 1956; emphasis added).

President David O. McKay gave us the key to making ourselves sensitive and receptive to the Lord's inspiration. First, we must feel calm and relaxed. Our minds cannot be filled with noise and chatter so that we cannot hear the inspiration when it comes. Second, we must feel right toward each other. If we are upset with family members, leaders at work, or neighbors, it is difficult to allow the subtle inspiration of the Spirit to dwell within us. On one occasion, Joseph Smith had difficulty translating by the Spirit of the Lord until he reconciled his feelings with his wife, Emma. And third, we must inquire about something, or as President McKay explained, be "thinking about the duties of the day." To let a concern or thought rest lightly upon the mind allows "impressions to come more clearly, as if to hear a voice."

The Lord admonishes us, further, to "study it out in your mind; then you must ask me if it be right, and if it is right I will cause that your bosom shall burn within you; therefore, you shall feel that it is right" (D&C 9:9).

Sometimes the inspiration comes in the morning. Other times it comes during the quiet evening hours. The location may also vary. Leaders have received inspiration walking to work, meditating in the temple, sitting under the tall trees of a forest. It is most important to keep ourselves calm and receptive to the inspiration and help of the Spirit of the Lord.

Joy in Service

Christ's demeanor was not characterized by a gloomy face nor a voice of deep sadness. He never ignored his followers' specific needs, nor did he give them an impression of extreme busyness. The Gospels record that Jesus easily and unhurriedly mingled with large crowds, small children, publicans, outcasts, rich, poor, Pharisees, merchants, and tax collectors. The scriptures also indicate that he talked with anyone who wanted to discuss points of law, to learn the gospel, or to obtain relief from physical affliction.

Jesus seemed to enjoy ministering to the needs of people. At times he was criticized because he found joy and peace in serving and because his disciples did not fast in order to look appropriately gloomy. "Scribes and Pharisees murmured against his disciples, saying, Why do ye eat and drink with publicans and sinners?" They questioned Jesus further, "Why do the disciples of John fast often, and make prayers, and likewise the disciples of the Pharisees; but thine eat and drink?" (Luke 5:30, 33).

Jesus' answer is a marvelous description of how he perceived his own mission. "Can ye make the children of the bridechamber fast, while the bridegroom is with them? But the days will come, when the bridegroom shall be taken away from them, and then shall they fast in those days" (Luke 5:34–35). Jesus seems to have been saying, "I am the bridegroom. Let us celebrate together and be happy now, for there will be sufficient time for solemnity when we are no longer together."

Happiness in leading comes from enjoying the moment, celebrating the now. Often a bishop sees only a long series of Sunday meetings ahead of him and an even longer list of duties to be completed. During and between meetings, a leader must understand that he or she is dealing with people who have individual needs. People retain their individual identities, even when sitting together in a meeting. One person needs a smile, another a handshake, a third a word of encouragement, and a fourth a little direction.

A leader is a sign of hope whose ideas are worth following. If a leader feels that the main goal is to complete a specific number of meetings, the experience of being a leader is likely to be somewhat depressing. On the other hand, if a leader sees a meeting as an opportunity to attend to the needs of various people, encourage them, and give them information that allows them to be happier and more successful during the coming week, then both the leader and the followers are lifted up and rejoice together.

The leader's goal should be to help people achieve something, not just hold a meeting, conduct an interview, or make a visit. Jesus, as a great leader, enjoyed walking through fields, matching wits, eating, and having long conversations with people. He is the perfect example of a leader ministering to people first and administering programs and procedures second. Jesus is a leader bearing glad tidings of great joy, bringing good news, and describing a life-style calculated to lighten the hearts and minds of all his followers.

In Jesus' time being a shepherd was a well-respected and dignified vocation. Jesus approved of the role of a true shepherd: "Verily, verily, I say unto you, He that entereth not by the door into the sheepfold, but climbeth up some other way, the same is a thief and a robber. But he that entereth in by the door is the shepherd of the sheep" (John 10:1–2).

Jesus pointed out the difference between a real shepherd and a hireling shepherd. The hireling sees the sheep as a flock. The shepherd knows each member of the flock by name. The hireling flees as the wolf approaches the sheep, while the shepherd defends them and lays down his life, if necessary. The shepherd has a personal interest and love for each mem-

85

ber of his flock. As a leader, Jesus declared, "I am the good shepherd, and know my sheep, and am known of mine" (John 10:14).

Emphasize the Spirit of the Law

Jesus often set aside the narrow forms and practices of the Pharisees. He constantly deemphasized the letter of the law and gave renewed life to the spirit of the law. "Walk so far on the Sabbath," said the rule and the tradition. Jesus walked as far as he needed.

"Pray in this way and in these public places." Jesus was outraged. He pleaded, "Pray to thy Father which is in secret; and thy Father which seeth in secret shall reward thee openly" (Matthew 6:6).

"Eat these things and these you shall not," said the code. Knowing certain foods were good for the body, Jesus pointed out a greater truth: "Not that which goeth into the mouth defileth a man; but that which cometh out of the mouth, this defileth a man" (Matthew 15:11).

There are very few instances in which the Lord tells us how to do anything specifically. For instance, "Remember the sabbath day, to keep it holy" is a guideline without a long list of do's and don'ts (Exodus 20:8). "Honour thy father and thy mother" is a great principle with a wonderful promise: "that thy days may be long upon the land which the Lord thy God giveth thee" (Exodus 20:12). But no extensive list of practices and procedures is given to implement the principle.

Every leadership meeting has a distinct purpose. That principle is important for leaders to understand. Bishopric meetings are planning meetings. Executive meetings are primarily to carry out the plans from bishopric meetings. Correlation meetings are a time to focus the full power of the ward on one individual or one family. Family home evening is a time for gospel principles to be personalized for each member of the family and for family concerns to be resolved.

The outcome of the meeting is much more important than the procedure used. The meeting length, number of agenda items, and order of reports are not as critical as accomplishing the purpose of the meeting.

To be great leaders, we should focus on the results achieved, not on the number of meetings held or the specific procedures used. Effective leadership is measured by the quality of results achieved, not by the amount of effort expended.

As leaders we need to be careful, however, about how we apply various programs and procedures to our followers. Each lesson, program, and general policy should produce the greatest benefit for the person to whom it is applied. Minor adjustments may be necessary. Lessons given during priesthood quorum meetings, for example, should be adapted to the needs of quorum members. As the guidelines for quorum leaders suggest, "teaching in each quorum meeting is directed toward the particular needs of your quorum members and is in harmony with the teachings of the Church. If a particular need exists that is not covered in the current manual, you may use previous study guides, conference addresses, and scriptures. Prayerful discernment coupled with information gained in personal priesthood interviews will guide you in selecting lesson topics. . . . Discussing personal applications of the concepts presented and how members can teach them to their families should occupy the greater portion of the lesson time" (*Melchizedek Priesthood Personal Study Guide 1989*, pp. xi–xii).

Home teaching messages need to be carefully adapted to the specific needs of individual families. Home teachers take the message of the First Presidency from the current *Ensign* magazine to their respective families. Some home teachers go out near the end of the month, spend only a few minutes with their families, and use the entire time reading aloud. On one occasion, a home teacher visited a family that consisted of a mother, who looked a bit worn out, and her three small children. The home teacher read a paragraph or two and then explained that it was important to build a worldwide church, but the children did not seem particularly interested. They were attempting to make friends at the elementary school where they were newly enrolled. At no time did the home teacher consider the concerns of this family and relate the First Presidency's message to their immediate situation.

President Ezra Taft Benson, in a special presentation, encouraged mothers to make every effort to avoid leaving their children in order to work outside the home. After the message was delivered, bishops and stake presidents received inquiries from some working mothers who were concerned about being unable to remain at home with their children. Although they knew the principle is true, it seemed impossible for them to follow it immediately. Local leaders helped concerned individuals work out their own solutions: mothers who did not have an income sufficient for their family's needs would work as necessary, enlist the support of others to help their children, and plan ways to make the transition into staying at home with their children. This process illustrates how leaders, with the guidance of the Spirit, help their followers live the law.

Avoid the Appearance of Busyness

For more than three years, Jesus walked confidently in and out of towns, cities, and places where people gathered.

He did not act as a stern ruler, rigid judge, or vain leader. He was an empathic friend and servant to all, seeking to lift the hearts of people and to help them to find joy in daily living.

He resisted the appearance of busyness. Nowhere can we find scriptural evidence that Jesus raced from place to place or hurried from one task to another. Indeed, the evidence suggests that the Savior spent time with each person or group who gathered around him (Luke 7:36; Luke 9:12).

As President David O. McKay toured the various missions in the Pacific, he was greeted by throngs of people and numerous missionaries. His ability to separate the crowd into clusters of individuals and spend a little time with each person who pressed close to him was uncanny and instructive. He never seemed too busy and rushed to say hello and greet people. On one occasion, after welcoming hundreds of government officials, local church leaders, and members, President McKay finally made his way to mission headquarters. He was immediately surrounded by missionaries and mission home staff. He shook the hand of each missionary, looked the missionary in the eye and inquired, "What is your name?" For a moment, it seemed that the whole world disappeared. There were only two people standing and looking into each other's eyes. The prophet seemed to see much deeper than the eye, almost into the center of the person's life.

Sometimes the missionaries failed to remember their own names. President McKay would chuckle and wait. Finally, when a name was blurted out, he would quietly ask where the missionary was from. Then he would ask, "Do you know the McMillans?" or some family name, or he would inquire about how the missionary work was going and offer a suggestion and brief counsel. Though President

McKay had a hectic daily agenda, he never gave the appearance of busyness. He took the time to show individuals that their leader was not too busy for his followers.

When the children swarmed around Jesus, tugging at him and touching him, the disciples thought their actions were improper and tried to stop them, but Jesus quickly reminded them, "Suffer the little children to come unto me, and forbid them not: for of such is the kingdom of God" (Mark 10:14). Jesus had time for the little children, just as President Spencer W. Kimball had time for the prisoners at the Utah state prison. When he visited, they wanted to shake his hand and have their pictures taken with him.

An important way to avoid the appearance of being rushed is to allow for extra time to travel to a place or complete a task. A bishop who rushes into sacrament meeting a few minutes late and ignores the congregation in order to get the meeting started is probably not allowing enough time for the interviews that made him late in the first place. Contrast that with the bishop who finishes his tasks ten minutes early and is able to greet the families of the ward when they come to church. At the appropriate time, the bishop moves, unrushed, toward the front of the chapel, shakes hands with a few more people, relaxes, takes a deep breath, and enjoys conducting the meeting.

Christ seems to have set a comfortable but steady pace for accomplishing his work. In modern scriptures the Lord admonishes us not to run faster or labor more than we have the strength for but to be diligent to the end (D&C 10:4). Jesus emphasized getting results rather than giving the appearance of busyness. Some leaders mistakenly believe that to be busy is to be effective. These leaders focus on the effort rather than on the result.

In the great missionary work of the Church, elders and

sisters must not become too preoccupied with the number of hours spent in scripture study, tracting, or presenting discussions. The focus of the missionary should be on helping investigators to understand and accept the gospel message, be baptized into the Church, and receive the companionship of the Holy Ghost.

When we focus on results, our labors usually become more directed. Our traditional missionary approaches may be shortened considerably, especially if the Lord intervenes and prepares the person to more quickly become a member of the Church. As leaders we try to help someone in the ward who is inactive by focusing on how to immediately activate the person, rather than spending a lot of time strategizing or having various members stop by and visit the individual. Perhaps the leader should simply ask the individual to help on a ward project or "meet me at the church Sunday, and I will introduce you to some tremendous sisters in the Relief Society." A direct approach is often a more efficient way to focus on results.

Enjoy One Thing at a Time

Jesus made many decisions about his priorities. On one occasion Jesus was going to the house of the ruler of the synagogue because the ruler's daughter "lay a dying" (Luke 8:42). As he walked along, the multitude crowded about him, and Jesus perceived that "virtue [was] gone out of [him]" when someone touched him (Luke 8:46). He stopped and asked who it was. A woman, perceiving that she had been noticed, "came trembling" to him to confess that she had touched him and had been immediately healed. Jesus took time out of his journey to speak with her, comfort her, and explain that "thy faith hath made thee whole" (Luke 8:48).

A very busy executive was making phone calls, but he made the calls a little differently from the way most people make them. He paused before he dialed. He thought about the person he was calling next and the purpose of the call. He also tried to remember when he had last talked to that person and what opening comments would communicate friendliness and helpfulness. For a moment, all other calls were forgotten. It was a time to be happy, in this moment, with this individual. The executive was quite relaxed and ready to enjoy the call.

All too often we don't stop to think about enjoying a morning stretch, a little conversation, or even the sun on our necks. We are so occupied with going places and doing things that we sometimes fail to enjoy the actual trip or the specific task. For instance, if we would take a moment to relax while we are drinking a glass of water, feel it touching our tongue, taste it, and focus on it going down our throats and refreshing us, the water could be as enjoyable as a serving of turkey or mashed potatoes.

While Jesus conversed with the woman who had been healed by touching the hem of his garment, someone from the ruler's house said to the ruler, "Thy daughter is dead; trouble not the Master." But when Jesus heard it, he explained that if they believed, she would be made whole. Then Jesus went to the house and invited Peter, James, John, and the maiden's mother and father to come inside. They "laughed him to scorn" when he told them that the maiden was not dead, so Jesus invited them to leave, took the maiden by the hand, and said, "Maid, arise." She arose, and Jesus asked the parents to give her something to eat (Luke 8:49–55).

Sometimes we become so busy as leaders that we constantly think about all the things we have to accomplish and fail to enjoy the task at hand. It takes discipline to focus, but, like Jesus, we can render service and truly enjoy each opportunity.

Some home teachers complained about the drudgery of visiting families each month who are doing so well that they don't need a visit. In those cases the home teachers should consult with the parents about questions and concerns of the family members. Their efforts should center on responding to specific needs. They could, for example, find answers to questions. Helping a child by sharing an instructive story or challenging someone to do something better can make a visit really enjoyable. Home teachers should focus on each family and their own specific contribution to the family.

Between the first days of Jesus' ministry, when shouting crowds hailed the new prophet-leader, to the last hours of his mortal agony on the cross, this perfect leader never allowed himself to sink into, or remain in, the dismal abyss of despair and desperation. Time after time, Jesus was renewed and strengthened by his adherence to the laws of health, his magnificent faith, constant prayer, and finding happiness in service by responding to the specific needs of individuals.

We have the same opportunities to be strengthened and renewed as we attempt to influence and lead our families, Church members, neighbors, and co-workers. Our goal is to help all people think more nobly about themselves and reach their godlike potential. To maintain our strength, hope, and happiness over an extended time, we must serve the Lord, learn more about daily self-renewal, and claim the promises made in Isaiah: "But they that wait upon the Lord shall renew their strength; they shall mount up with wings as eagles; they shall run, and not be weary; and they shall walk and not faint" (Isaiah 40:31).

7

ACHIEVING THE CHALLENGE OF PERFECT LEADERSHIP

We have now come full circle in our quest to understand how to become better leaders. The ideal leader is Jesus Christ himself, and the ideal leadership style is Christlike. Are we ready to accept the challenge of Jesus to "Come, follow me" and practice Christlike leadership at home, at work, in church, and in the community?

All of us are leaders. Whenever we influence others to move toward a goal, we are acting as leaders. We have been leaders in the past, and we will continue to be leaders in the future. Leadership is not necessarily a function of a specific work position, family role, or church calling. It is a way of getting work done and handling responsibilities. Indeed, leadership may even be considered a way of life.

Jesus Christ and his followers changed the history of the world. Reading the story of his perfect leadership reveals that Christ succeeded by empowering his disciples with great faith in accomplishing the work at hand. This endowment of power and understanding not only produced magnificent achievement in his immediate disciples but in their successors as well.

Like the early disciples of Christ, we have the same

opportunity to realize our own leadership potentials. "One of the great teachings of the Man of Galilee, the Lord Jesus Christ, was that you and I carry within us immense possibilities. In urging us to be perfect as our Father in Heaven is perfect, Jesus was not taunting us or teasing us. He was telling us a great truth about our possibilities and potentials. It is a truth almost too stunning to contemplate" (Spencer W. Kimball, "The Perfect Executive," p. 7). Furthermore, Jesus is "the perfect Example and Leader, not asking us to do what he has not done, not asking us to endure what he has not endured, giving us enough, but not more than we can manage. I thank him who did everything perfectly for sharing his precious work with those of us who then do it so imperfectly. I testify that he and the Father are serious about stretching our souls in this second estate. I thank him for truly teaching us about our personal possibilities and for divinely demonstrating directions — not just pointing" (Neal A. Maxwell, "Jesus of Nazareth, Savior and King," *Ensign*, Mar. 1976, p. 27).

We Grow Through Daily Experiences

Christ's disciples had difficulty early in their ministry in trying to follow the example of their great leader. The scriptures record an incident in which the disciples were not able to heal a young man who was foaming at the mouth and gnashing his teeth. Jesus reproved the disciples for their lack of faith. He then healed the youth and later instructed his disciples: "This kind can come forth by nothing, but prayer and fasting" (Mark 9:29).

These same disciples continued to grow and develop. As they did so, they gained the faith and confidence necessary to heal a man who was lame from birth. Peter and John said, "In the name of Jesus Christ of Nazareth rise up and walk." Immediately the man stood up and started walking and leaping, praising God (see Acts 3:1–7).

We all accept our leadership opportunities with considerable fear and trembling. Sleepless nights often follow the calling of a new Relief Society leader or quorum president. General authorities of the Church are not immune to the feeling of weakness, especially when they contemplate the extent of their new responsibilities.

Most parents constantly worry about how well they lead their children and whether they are effectively influencing their children to choose righteousness. We can become great leaders and valued friends by exerting a positive influence in our families, church callings, and work activities. Consequently, we need to follow the example of Jesus.

Christ is the cornerstone of religious conviction. A person untouched by the words and deeds of Christ lacks the element that engenders great and noble leadership. We need constantly to keep Jesus Christ in the foreground of our daily living. We need to let him be the light by which we see the way. Each of us must reflect the character of Christ by adopting his words and deeds in our own lives. As Christ lived and led, so must we also live and lead.

In these pages, we have attempted to illuminate the essence of Christ's leadership through his deeds and teachings. Five essential keys to Christlike leadership have been identified and discussed. These keys can serve as a guide to personal growth. For example, young people can retain these principles in their minds and let the principles guide them as they grow into leadership roles. These keys can balance their lives and eliminate incongruities between how they act at school, at work, at home, and at church. As a way to keep hopes and dreams alive, the Christlike leadership approach represents a tried and true way to succeed.

For those who now occupy leadership positions, the keys to Christlike leadership may point out areas of weakness where a little improvement could result in big gains. Our experience with leaders is that most have unknowingly given little attention to at least three of the five areas.

To help you accept the challenge of Christlike leadership and start adding to your present leadership abilities, following is a summary of the five keys to leadership success.

Treat Others as Friends

The greatest gift we can give ourselves is to become transformed into Christ's friends. The greatest gift we can give others is to help them become similarly transformed. If we let the Savior's words abide in us, if we love one another, and if we follow his perfect leadership example, we can have the ennobling experiences that he had and become his friends. Then we can go forward as the Savior did and help to heal and transform others. "Herein," says Jesus, "is my Father glorified, that ye bear much fruit; so shall ye be my disciples" (John 15:8).

When we genuinely treat others as friends, they tend to like us and be influenced by what we say and do. Hence, treating others as friends enhances our leadership effectiveness. In a leadership seminar, a businessman asked, "But how do you treat someone as a friend?" The instructor answered the participant's question by asking everyone in the room to close their eyes and imagine a long hallway. "Now imagine that one of your good friends has been away on a trip for two weeks," he said. "As you look up from your end of the hallway, imagine that your friend has just come into view from the other end of the hallway. See yourself and your friend walking toward each other and stopping next to each other. Watch what you do and say."

Then the seminar instructor asked the participants to explain what they said and did when they met their friends in the hallway. "I smiled and talked enthusiastically about where she had been and what she had been doing," said one woman. "We laughed and hugged," said another. "I asked if he needed any help and suggested that he come over to supper that evening so that we could talk longer," said a man.

After numerous responses, the message became quite clear: Treat others as you treat your best friends. Say hello. Smile. Ask questions that express your interest in them. Ask what they are doing. Express appreciation for them. Be of service. Encourage them. And don't be afraid to walk, work, eat, and dream together.

We must remember that the people we meet in stores, offices, restaurants, parks, and other places are the very people we are expected to love and serve. It is useless to think that we are all noble sons and daughters of Heavenly Father if we can't treat each other as brothers and sisters and genuine friends.

Create a Positive Force

Good leaders are never dull. They create a feeling that things are moving in a positive way. They demonstrate by their walk and their talk that they are filled with quiet confidence and great strength. They unleash the total power of their personalities.

Each of us must develop our own positive force. Like the Savior, we need to decide what things we will be enthusiastically committed to, we will see that followers are treated compassionately, and we will lead with encouragement and a positive attitude.

Sister Carmen Sanchez was called to be a Relief Society

leader in a university ward. She was young, somewhat inexperienced, and very nervous about the calling. During the first meeting, attendance was low and the young sisters who did attend did not respond well to the lesson. Carmen was determined, however, to make things better. She committed herself to making her Relief Society the best in the stake. She became friends with all the members. She talked with them about their needs and about their future aspirations. She made her comments positive and encouraging.

Sister Sanchez soon built a loving relationship with each sister in Relief Society. The young sisters began to attend meetings and became more involved in the lessons. Carmen may not have understood all the principles that contributed to "perfect leadership," but she did create a positive force.

When leaders fail to create a strong force, lethargy usually sets in among their followers. Unfortunately, people follow the path of least resistance, slow down, and quickly become disenchanted. Being positive and encouraging when things are not going well is difficult. Effective leaders, however, have no other choice.

Invite Others to Follow

If there are no followers, there is no leader. A leader may want to lead and even be appointed to lead, but the ability to attract followers initially determines whether the leader will be successful. Leadership theories assume that if we want to attract followers, we must prepare ourselves to inspire them by creating an attractive vision of what can be achieved and then motivate them by continually and vividly showing that vision. Finally, the leader confidently invites others to unite in achieving the vision.

All of us like to follow leaders who have made the kind of achievements we would like to make and who rejoice in their accomplishments. Christ spent his whole life describing a joyful life-style that helps lighten the burdens of mankind. Faith, repentence, baptism, and the gift of the Holy Ghost were the messages he exhorted over and over to everyone who would listen.

"Come, follow me," Jesus implored. He is the light, the living water, the way. He urged us to be perfect as our Father in Heaven is perfect. He wanted us to have the power to do the things that he did. The vision that Christ presents to the people is magnificent. Millions are attracted to him and his ideas. Indeed, on occasion, they have wanted him not only to be their leader but to be their king.

To attract followers to a cause in any field of endeavor, we must see beyond the immediate activities of the day. We must plant our feet firmly on the earth and then reach toward the stars to find a dream that excites people to action.

As leaders, we are responsible for our followers, and unless we know where we are going, we will not get there nor will our followers. Goals help us implement our vision. Goals are statements of what needs to be done to achieve the vision. One way to create a goal is to identify a concern that is bothersome or uncomfortable. Think of something about your family that concerns you. Perhaps you think your family members are not kind enough to one another. In other words, you may feel uncomfortable that family members do not act kindly often enough to one another.

Next, turn your concern into a goal by deciding with your spouse and children what each individual family member should do to show more kindness to family members. Each person in the family, for example, might compliment or do an act of service for another family member sometime during the next month. The concern has been turned into a goal by stating what you would do to alleviate the concern.

Giving a gift shows kindness; thus, your goal is to have everyone give someone else a gift of thoughtfulness or service.

The very same procedure can be used in the business world. Say to yourself, "Right now, my main concern with the company is that we are not providing adequate customer service." Decide with the help of other employees how to overcome your concern. The answer will be a goal that will eliminate the concern and lead the company to achieve the vision. The goal might read: each employee will perform one or more acts of customer service each day.

Your next step is to invite as many people as possible to be involved in achieving the goal. Then do what the Savior did: speak and instruct with great diligence and patience until everyone understands. Be sure to ask questions to confirm their understanding and listen to questions to confirm your own understanding. If our goals, dreams, and visions are attractive to people, they will want to join in and reap the rewards.

Empower Followers to Act

Have you ever had the experience of telling children, "Just as soon as family home evening is over, you can go ahead and bake some delicious chocolate chip cookies"? After the closing prayer, with a twinkle in their eyes and grinning ear to ear, they dash into the kitchen. They can already taste the warm cookies melting in their mouths. But usually, in less than a minute, they are back, realizing that they don't know where to begin or what to do. The goal is clear, but its implementation cannot occur until they receive more specific details.

Lofty goals without ways to achieve them are not useful. Individuals must be invited to participate in determining goals and then be instructed in how to help achieve the goals. First, delegate activities that lead to the accomplishment of the goals. Give each person a specific assignment. Discuss the best ways to do the assignment so that it will most likely be completed. Ask each individual to describe what should be done and when.

Second, invite all persons, individually, to begin. Express your appreciation for their involvement and willingness to accept the assignment. Indicate how soon the assignment needs to be completed and have them give you a progress report. Do not be afraid to encourage them to take full responsibility for seeing that the assignment is completed on time.

When disapproval needs to be expressed, do it with charity, clarity, and specificity. Focus on aspects of the assignment that were not completed rather than on the person. Show forth an increase in love toward the person reproved (D&C 121:43).

The leader's task is to involve as many people as possible. Everyone should do something in order to feel the excitement and share the thrill of successfully completing a project. The leader empowers followers to act by staying close to them. We should emulate Christ's example by not being afraid to eat, walk, work, and laugh together, as friends, with those whom we are asked to lead.

Strengthen Yourself

It is not easy always to be positive when we attempt to lead others. To follow the example of him who constantly encouraged us to "be of good cheer" can be accomplished only if we pay proper attention to the sources of physical and spiritual strength. Physical fitness is a subject of great interest in countries all around the world. Physiologists unanimously agree that regular exercise tends to help people respond better to everyday stresses.

A good conditioning program for most people should raise the heart beat above one hundred beats per minute for twenty minutes, three or four times a week. Brisk walking, jogging, cycling, dancing, swimming, and participating in a competitive sport are all useful ways of strengthening our bodies.

All the benefits of regular exercise are reduced considerably without good nutrition and proper rest. We also need to avoid harmful substances like caffeine, nicotine, alcohol, and all mind- and emotion-altering drugs.

Leaders should not only get appropriate exercise, rest, and nutrition, but they should also develop a balanced pattern of living. Hypertense people and workaholics tend to have more health problems, especially heart disease. Perhaps the Savior's example of walking outdoors, and engaging in social, family, intellectual, and spiritual activities, is a good one for us to follow.

Remember, the goal is not to compound problems by adding more undertakings to our already busy lives. Rather, the goal is to develop a better balance among our daily activities. Our ultimate goal is to focus on one event, allow extra time, and really enjoy it.

Spiritual strength comes from exercising our faith in the Savior and applying it to an important work or calling. In fact, an overwhelming faith can control and calm adverse circumstances that impede our progress toward worthy goals.

Great spiritual strength comes through prayer, listening to our Heavenly Father, and being sensitive to the still, small voice. This divine communication is critical in learning how to lead as the Perfect Leader led, because Jesus left neither detailed rules nor ready references to be used in all leadership situations.

President Ezra Taft Benson reminded us that "usually the Lord gives us the overall objectives to be accomplished and some guidelines to follow, but he expects us to work out most of the details and methods. The methods and procedures are usually developed through study and prayer and by living so that we can obtain and follow the promptings of the Spirit" (in Conference Report, Apr. 1965, p. 121).

Imagine that it is early morning, and the sun is just beginning to glitter on the surface of the sea as the fishermen strain to cast their nets into the water. Beads of perspiration appear on their foreheads as they toil. A lone, solitary figure strolls along the shore, intently studying their activities. As he nears their place of work, he says, "Hello, Peter and Andrew. I am in need of good men to assist in the work of the gospel. Follow me, and I will make you fishers of men." They immediately dropped their nets and followed him.

As they followed Jesus without hesitation, so we may also. They shared in his vision of eternal life. They grew by his constant direction and drew from his boundless energy. They were enlivened by his conviction and dynamic communication and ennobled by his patient and enduring instruction. As leaders we, too, may do the same.

The coming years promise great challenges and opportunities for us in every leadership responsibility. Elder John E. Carmack, executive director of the Church Historical Department, has observed that "the Church and individuals will thrive if they turn problems into opportunities and grow. We will need to be careful of our resources, simplify our procedures, have more independence, and do things of our own free will and choice" (Dell Van Orden and Gerry Avant, *Church News*, 13 Jan. 1990, p. 7). With the help of our

Lord and Savior, we will meet our challenges and unparalled opportunities as mothers and fathers, as teachers and leaders in this remarkable era. Though the tempests rage about us and the waves crest and fall, let us courageously follow the example of our perfect leader. Let us hear again in our own hearts, as his faithful followers heard it on the Sea of Galilee, the voice of the Master whispering to us, "It is I, Jesus. Be not afraid."

REFERENCES

Ashton, Wendell J. "Thanksgiving: Kindness in Japan," *Instructor*, Nov. 1961, back cover.

Benson, Ezra Taft. In Conference Report, Apr. 1965, p. 121.

———. In Conference Report, Oct. 1974, p. 92.

BYU Today, Nov. 1989, p. 34.

Editors of *Campus Life* Magazine. *Reach Out*. Wheaton, Ill.: Tyndale House Foundation, 1967.

Kimball, Spencer W. "The Perfect Executive," address given to the Young Presidents Organization, Sun Valley, Idaho, 15 Jan. 1977.

Kimball, Spencer W. "Jesus: The Perfect Leader," *Ensign*, Aug. 1979, p. 5.

Lee, Harold B. Address to LDS seminary and institute teachers, Brigham Young University, Provo, Utah, 6 July 1956.

Maxwell, Neal A. "Jesus of Nazareth, Savior and King," *Ensign*, Mar. 1976, p. 27.

McKay, David O. *Gospel Ideals*. Salt Lake City, Utah: Improvement Era, 1953.

———. *Man May Know for Himself*. Comp. Clare Middlemiss. Salt Lake City, Utah: Deseret Book Co., 1969.

Melchizedek Priesthood Personal Study Guide 1989. Salt Lake City, Utah: The Church of Jesus Christ of Latter-day Saints, 1988.

Richards, Stephen L. In Conference Report, Apr. 1949, p. 141.

Romney, Marion G. "What Would Jesus Do?" *New Era*, Sept. 1972, p. 5.

REFERENCES

Russell, W.H. *Christ the Leader*. Milwaukee: Bruce Publishing Co., 1937.

Smith, Joseph. *Lectures on Faith*. Salt Lake City, Utah: Deseret Book Co., 1985.

———. *Teachings of the Prophet Joseph Smith*. Sel. Joseph Fielding Smith. Salt Lake City, Utah: Deseret Press, 1938.

Spafford, Belle S. *Women in Today's World*. Salt Lake City, Utah: Deseret Book Co., 1971.

Talmage, James E. *Jesus the Christ*. Salt Lake City, Utah: Deseret Book Co., 1973.

Tanner, N. Eldon. "The Message," *New Era*, June 1977, p. 4.

Taylor, John. *The Gospel Kingdom*. Comp. G. Homer Durham. Salt Lake City, Utah: Bookcraft, 1944.

Van Orden, Dell, and Gerry Avant. "Church Gears Up," *Church News*, 13 Jan. 1990, p. 7.

INDEX